More advance praise for *Focal Point*:

"Brian Tracy has done it again: He's written the authoritative guide to personal effectiveness. In the age of distraction, *Focal Point* will show you how to focus on what really matters to produce the results that really count."

—Mark Sanborn, speaker and author of *Upgrade!*
Proven Strategies for Dramatically Increasing
Personal and Professional Success

"I couldn't have written it better myself!"

—Lee Iacocca, retired Chairman,
Chrysler Corporation

"This book is *invaluable!* Get it. Consume it. Live it! My business and personal results have been dramatically improved. Yours can be too!"

—Ty Boyd, founder,
The Excellence in Speaking Institute

"*Focal Point* hits the bull's-eye. In typical Brian Tracy style, this isn't some pep-talk motivational "you can do it" book; this is the real step-by-step stuff. You can't miss when you follow this proven system. Most importantly, *Focal Point* is an owner's manual for fulfilling life, not just a get-rich system . . . though you'll certainly achieve abundant wealth by implementing this practical strategy."

—George R. Walther, author,
What You Say Is What You Get With
Power Talking

"The more successful you are, the more you need this book. The major choice today is between the good, better, and best activities and decisions about time. This book helps you cut through the clutter to the core opportunities!"

—Dianna Booher, author, *E-Writing,*
Communicate With Confidence and
Get a Life Without Sacrificing Your Career

"Brian Tracy is the world's leading authority on getting results in your life. No other individual has studied and taught the techniques to help you achieve your true potential as much as Brian Tracy. The best of his studies are in this book. You owe it to yourself to read it."

—Patricia Fripp, CSP, CPAE; author,
Get What You Want; past President,
National Speakers Association

"*Focal Point* is articulated genius converging the synergy of focus, goal setting, time management, and strategic planning to leverage personal presence, persona, and power for significance in life and living."

—Naomi Rhode, CSP, CPAE Speaker Hall of
Fame; past President, National Speakers
Association; cofounder, Smart Practice

"Tracy again delivers his amazing sense of relevance in *Focal Point*. His goal is unabashedly large — answers on how to achieve success without sacrificing a balanced and happy life — and he meets it admirably. No one else writing today is as skillful in supporting intelligent advice with meaningful examples that 'strike home' and compel the kind of change that leads to happiness — self-directed change."

—Jim Tunney, Ed.D.; coauthor, *Chicken Soup for the Sports Fan's Soul*

"Personal success and Brian Tracy are synonymous. Nobody I know can teach you more about how to achieve and succeed than Brian. He makes the case clearly and then proves it in his own remarkable life. If he recommends it, do it. He knows what he's talking about."

— Jim Cathcart, author, *The Acorn Principle*

"Brian Tracy's poignant counsel and lucid insights provide us with the formula for personal and professional success that is both scientifically accurate, and yet practical."

—Edwin J. Feulner, Ph.D.; President, The Heritage Foundation

Focal Point

Focal Point

A Proven System to Simplify Your Life, Double
Your Productivity, and Achieve All Your Goals

Brian Tracy

AMACOM
American Management Association

New York • Atlanta • Chicago • Kansas City • San Francisco • Washington, D. C.
Brussels • Toronto • Mexico City • Tokyo

Special discounts on bulk quantities of AMACOM books are available to corporations, professional associations, and other organizations. For details, contact Special Sales Department, AMACOM, a division of American Management Association, 1601 Broadway, New York, NY 10019.
Tel.: 212-903-8316   Fax: 212-903-8083
Web site: www.amacombooks.org

This publication is designed to provide accurate and authoritative information in regard to the subject matter covered. It is sold with the understanding that the publisher is not engaged in rendering legal, accounting, or other professional service. If legal advice or other expert assistance is required, the services of a competent professional person should be sought.

Library of Congress Cataloging-in-Publication Data

Tracy, Brian, 1944–
    Focal point: a proven system to simplify your life, double your productivity, and achieve all your goals / Brian Tracy.
        p. cm.
    Includes index.
    ISBN 0-8144-7129-3
        1. Success—psychological aspects. 2. Success in business. I. Title.
BF637.S8 T635 2001
158—dc21   2001046150

Printing number
10 9 8 7 6

*This book is dedicated to my dear friend and
business partner, Vic Conant, a fine man,
a tremendous support in good times and bad,
and a never-ending source of optimism,
intelligence, and common sense.*

Contents

Focal Point

Introduction

Once upon a time, there was a major technical problem at a nuclear power plant. This malfunction was slowing energy generation and reducing the efficiency of the entire operation.

As much as they tried, the plant's engineers could not identify and solve the problem. So they brought in one of the nation's top consultants on nuclear power plant construction and engineering to see whether he could determine what was wrong. The consultant arrived, put on a white coat, took his clipboard, and went to work. For the next two days, he walked around, studying the hundreds of dials and gauges in the control room, taking notes, and making calculations.

At the end of the second day, he took a black felt marker out of his pocket, climbed up on a ladder, and put a large black "X" on one of the gauges.

"This is the problem," he explained. "Repair and replace the apparatus connected to this meter, and the problem will be solved."

He then took off his white smock, drove back to the airport, and flew home. The engineers disassembled the apparatus and discovered that, sure enough, this was the cause of the problem. It was soon repaired, and the plant was back up to full capacity.

About a week later the plant manager received a bill from the consultant for $10,000 for "services rendered."

The plant manager was surprised at the size of the bill, even though this was a multibillion-dollar facility and the problem had been costing an enormous amount of money in lost generating capacity. After all, he reasoned, the consultant had come in, stood around for a couple of days, written a black "X" on one of the gauges, and then returned home. Ten thousand dollars seemed like a high fee for such a simple job.

The plant manager wrote back to the consultant, "We have received your bill. Could you please break down and itemize your charges? It seems that all you did was to write one 'X' on a single gauge. Ten thousand dollars appears to be excessive for this amount of work."

Some days later, the plant manager received a new invoice from the consultant. It said, "For placing 'X' on gauge: $1.00. For knowing which gauge to place 'X' on: $9,999."

This simple story illustrates the most important single principle of success, achievement, and happiness in life. Knowing where to put the "X" in each part of your life is the critical determinant of everything you accomplish.

This "X" is your focal point. This is the one thing you can do in that area, at any given moment, to get the best result possible. Your ability to choose the correct time, place, and activity to place your "X" on has a greater impact on your life than any other factor.

In this book, you will learn a practical, proven, and powerful process that you can apply in every area of your life to achieve better, faster, easier results than you ever imagined possible. Just as the sun's rays, focused through a magnifying glass, can create intense heat and fire, your intelligence and abilities, focused and concentrated on a few key activities, can enable you to accomplish much more than the average person can and in far less time. Just as the focused energy in a laser beam cuts through steel, your ability to choose the most vital element of any situation will enable you to perform at extraordinary levels in any endeavor.

This book answers some of the key questions you probably ask yourself regularly: "How can I get control of my time and my life? How can I achieve maximum success in my career and still achieve balance in my relationships and my personal life? How can I have it all and still be happy and fulfilled?"

We are living today in perhaps the best time in human history. There have never been more opportunities and possibilities for more people to accomplish more of their goals. The level of affluence has never been higher, the average life span has never been longer, the number of options available to you has never been greater, and the world situation, in terms of peace and prosperity, has never been more stable.

Meanwhile, the explosion of knowledge and technology in the last few years, combined with the increasing intensity of competition in all fields, has accelerated the rate of change. More and more, you have too much to do and too little time. Your responsibilities and obligations seem to pile up. There are never enough hours in the day.

You may be earning more money and doing better than you have ever done before. But you often feel overwhelmed with the demands of your job and your personal life. You may be working harder today than ever before, yet you are getting less and less satisfaction and enjoyment from what you do. This book gives you the solution to these unavoidable challenges of modern life.

Focal Point is based on more than twenty-five years of personal experience in business. This first-hand knowledge has been combined with extensive research into the habits and behaviors of men and women who accomplish much more than the average person in their personal and business lives. *Focal Point* starts with the question, "Why are some people more successful and effective than others?"

Focal Point answers this question. This book explains why and how some people accomplish more in each of the important areas of their lives. It shows you how you can accomplish more in your work while having much more time to spend on your personal activities.

Focal Point is a synthesis of the best ideas and strategies on personal management ever brought together in one place, in one easy-to-use plan. *Focal Point* shows you to how to organize and simplify your life in the seven critical areas that are essential for complete balance and peace of mind.

You learn how to develop goals and plans in each of the areas that are important to you. You learn how to set clear priorities among the competing demands on your time. You learn how to focus single-mindedly on the one thing you can do at any given time to achieve the best results possible in that area. You learn where to put the "X" in your life, minute by minute and hour by hour.

The central concept of *Focal Point* is clarity. In the pages ahead, you will learn how to develop clarity about who you are and what you really want. You will learn how to achieve your most important goals faster and easier than you can imagine today. You will learn how to tap into and use your personal powers at a higher level than ever before.

The results our clients achieve by applying these strategies to their lives and work are often amazing. Participants in our programs and others who apply these principles report rapid improvements in every area. They often double their incomes, reduce the number of hours they work each week, get control of their time and their lives, and dramatically improve the quality of their relationships with their families and other people.

All great truths are simple. The power of *Focal Point* is that it teaches you a series of timeless truths that have been discovered and rediscovered by effective, happy people throughout the ages. You learn a new way of thinking about yourself and your world. You learn how to answer the question, "What do I really want to do with my life?"

Essentially, there are only four different things you can do to improve the quality of your life and work:

1. You can do *more* of certain things. You can do more of the things that are of greater value to you and bring you greater rewards and satisfaction.

2. You can do *less* of certain things. You can deliberately decide to reduce or discontinue activities or behaviors that are not as helpful as other activities and behaviors or can actually be hurtful to you in accomplishing the things you want.

3. You can *start* to do things you are not doing at all today. You can make new choices, learn new skills, begin new projects or activities, or change the entire focus of your work or personal life.

4. You can *stop* doing certain things altogether. You can stand back and evaluate your life with new eyes. You can then decide to discontinue activities and behaviors that are no longer consistent with what you want and where you want to go.

....

In the pages ahead, you will learn how to think the way the most effective people think and to take the actions that the most effective people take. You will learn how to develop your own plan for achieving rapid results in each part of your life that is important to you. You will learn how to accomplish more in the next couple of years than many people accomplish in a lifetime.

There are almost no limits to what you can be, do, or have when you apply the *Focal Point* process to your life.

CHAPTER ONE

Unlock Your Full Potential

Every great man has become great, every successful man has succeeded, in proportion as he has confined his powers to one particular channel.

—ORISON SWETT MARDEN

You can dramatically improve the overall quality of your life far faster than you might think possible. All you need is the desire to change, the decision to take action, the discipline to practice the new behaviors you have chosen, and the determination to persist until you get the results you want.

Here is a story that illustrates this point. An insurance executive enrolled in my Advanced Coaching and Mentoring Program had been working six to seven days per week, ten to twelve hours per day, and had not taken a vacation in more than four years when he began the program. He was earning more than $100,000 per year, but he was unfit, overweight, highly stressed, and not at all satisfied with his life. He felt overwhelmed, with too much to do and too little time. He was hoping that, at a minimum, this program would give him some new time management techniques that he could use to increase his productivity and get his life under control.

From the first day, he learned and applied the Focal Point Process. Step by step, he analyzed each part of his work and personal life. He identified the areas where he was getting the best results and earning the most money. At the same time, he identified the areas that consumed an enormous amount of time but contributed very little to his real goals. He made a list of everything he was doing, and then he applied the zero-based thinking question to each activity: "Knowing what I know now, if I were not doing this now, would I start it up again today?"

He realized almost immediately that there were an enormous number of activities he was caught up in and responsibilities that he had taken on over the years that were contributing very little to his life and his real goals. He then set new goals for his work, his family, his health, his financial situation, and his life in general. He compared everything he was doing with his goals. He decided to do *more* of some things and *less* of other things and to *start* doing certain things and *stop* other activities altogether.

This executive had a wonderful quality possessed by all truly effective men and women I know. He was able to stand back, analyze his life, make specific decisions, and then follow through on those decisions. The result was that within three months, he had cut his work week from seven days to five days. He had refocused his efforts on the top 20 percent of his clients and organized his activities to acquire more clients in that same category. At the same time, he began reducing and cutting back on the amount of time he was spending with the 80 percent of his clients who contributed only 20 percent of his revenues. This enabled him to spend more of his time with the clients who provided most of his income.

With his work life simplified and streamlined, he refocused on his family. He began spending more time with his wife and children. First, they arranged to go away for a weekend vacation, something they had not done for years. A few weeks later, they took an entire week away from work and school. Within six months, he was taking one week off per month with his family.

Meanwhile, because of his increased focus on his most valuable clients, within a year his income increased by more than 300 percent. He was exercising regularly and had lost 22 pounds. By doing fewer things of higher value and discontinuing activities of lower value, he dramatically improved the quality of his life in every area in just a few months.

This story is not unique. I have heard it thousands of times, all over the country and all over the world. As soon as people begin to apply these principles in their daily lives, the results they get are often miraculous. Even they are amazed at the incredible differences that take place and how quickly their lives change for the better. And what they have done, you can do as well.

Double Your Income, Double Your Time Off

By applying the Focal Point Process to your life, you can double your income and double your time off. Many people achieve these twin goals in as little as thirty days.

When they hear this claim, most people are skeptical. They do not believe that it is possible to double their income and double their time off simultaneously. Most people are trapped in an old paradigm: They believe that the only way they can increase their incomes is by increasing the amount of work they do or the number of hours they work. In fact, many people feel guilty if they are not working almost to the point of exhaustion most of the time. However, this is an old way of thinking that leads inevitably to a physical, emotional, and spiritual dead end.

The world has changed dramatically, and we must change with it. In less than two generations, we have moved from the Industrial Age through the Service Age and into the Information Age. In the Information Age, knowledge has become the primary resource and the most valuable factor of production. We have moved from the Age of Manpower to the Age of Mindpower. In this new age, you are no longer rewarded for the hours you put in but for what you put into those hours.

Peter Drucker calls this the Age of the Knowledge Worker. The way you think and get results today is totally different from the way it might have been in the past. Today, you are paid for accomplishments, not activities. You are paid for outcomes rather than for inputs, or the number of hours you work. Your rewards are determined by the quality and quantity of results you achieve in your area of responsibility. This change in the paradigm of work opens up unlimited opportunities for creative people who recognize it and capitalize on it.

Double Your Value, Double Your Income

Would you like to double your income? Of course you would! The only question is, "How can you do it?" Here is a simple way, almost guaranteed to work.

First, identify the things you do that contribute the greatest value to you and your company. The 80/20 Rule tells you that 20 percent of your tasks contribute 80 percent or more of the value of all the things you do. What are the top 20 percent of your activities that account, or can account, for 80 percent or more of the value of your work?

Whatever your answer, from now on resolve to spend *more* of your time doing more of the tasks that contribute the greatest value and enable you to achieve the most important results possible for you.

Second, identify the activities in the bottom 80 percent, the lower-value, time-consuming tasks that contribute very little to your results. Resolve to downsize, delegate, and eliminate as many of them as possible, as quickly as you possibly can.

In no time at all, if you discipline yourself to practice this simple approach, your results and rewards will increase. By persisting in this way of working, you will become more and more productive. You will accomplish more and more. Your productivity, your performance, your output, and eventually your pay will increase and eventually double.

You will begin to complete more tasks of higher value. You will make a more valuable contribution. You will be respected and esteemed more highly by the people who can most help you in your career. You will be paid more because the value of your work will be greater than that of others who spend most of their time on lower-value activities. Because you will be getting twice as much done in the same amount of time, you can then increase or even double your time off with no loss of productivity. Your whole life will change for the better.

You Are Responsible

Implementing this simple formula is largely a matter of personal choice. It is very much up to you. No one else can make this decision for you, and nobody can make this decision other than you.

Among the most important personal choices you can make is to accept complete responsibility for everything you are and everything you will ever be. This is the great turning point in life. The acceptance of personal responsibility is what separates the superior person from the average person. Personal responsibility is the preeminent trait of leadership and the wellspring of high performance in every person in every situation.

Accepting complete responsibility for your life means that you refuse to make excuses or blame others for anything in your life that you're not happy about. You refuse, from this moment forward, to criticize others for any reason. You refuse to complain about your situation or about what has happened in the past. You eliminate all your if-onlys and what-ifs and focus instead on what you really want and where you are going.

This decision to accept complete responsibility for yourself, your life, and your results, with no excuses, is absolutely essential if you want to double your income and double your time off. From now on, no matter what happens, say to yourself, "I am responsible."

If you are not happy with any part of your life, say, "I am responsible" and get busy changing it. If something goes wrong, accept responsibility and begin looking for a solution. If you are not happy with your current income, accept responsibility and begin doing the things that are necessary for you to increase it. If you are not happy with the amount of time you are spending with your family, accept responsibility for that and begin doing something about it.

When you accept responsibility, you feel personally powerful. Accepting responsibility gives you a tremendous sense of control over yourself and your life. The more responsibility you accept, the more confidence and energy you have. The more responsibility you accept, the more capable and competent you feel.

Accepting responsibility is the foundation of high self-esteem, self-respect, and personal pride. Accepting personal responsibility lies at the core of the personality of every outstanding man or woman.

On the other hand, when you make excuses, blame other people, complain, or criticize, you give your power away. You weaken yourself and your resolve. You turn over control of your emotions to the people and situations you are blaming or complaining about.

You do not escape responsibility by attempting to pass it off onto other people. You are still responsible. But you give up a sense of control over your life. You begin to feel like a victim and see yourself as a victim. You become passive and resigned rather than powerful and proactive. Instead of feeling on top of your world, you feel as if the world is on top of you. This way of thinking leads you into a blind alley from which there is no escape. It is a dead-end road on which you should refuse to travel.

See Yourself as Self-Employed

When you accept complete responsibility for your life, you begin to view yourself as self-employed, no matter who signs your paycheck. You see yourself as the president of your own personal service corporation. You see yourself as an entrepreneur heading a company with one employee: you. You see yourself as responsible for selling one product—your personal services—in a competitive marketplace. You see yourself as completely responsible for every element of your work, for production, quality control, training, development, communication, strategy, productivity improvement, and finances. You refuse to make excuses. Instead, you make progress.

Your personal company, or any company, can increase its profits in one or more of three ways. First, the company can increase its sales and revenues, holding costs constant. Second, the company can decrease its costs, holding sales and revenues constant. Third, the company can do something else altogether, where one or both of the first two are possible. As the president of your own company, you have these three options.

In the Focal Point Process, you identify the few things you can do that are more valuable and important than all the others. You then discipline yourself to focus all your energy and attention on those specific tasks. You say "no" to any activity or demand on your time that is not consistent with the most valuable work you can possibly be doing at that moment. You are responsible.

Whatever You Concentrate On Grows

Life is the study of attention. Where your attention goes, your heart goes also. Your ability to divert your attention from activities of lower value to activities of higher value is central to everything you accomplish in life.

In 1928, at the Hawthorne Electric Plant of General Electric, a group of time and motion experts conducted a series of experiments aimed at increasing the productivity of workers based on varying the working conditions and the environment in the plant.

The researchers selected a group of women who worked on a production line assembling motors. They explained to the women that they were going to be experimenting to find the best combination of working conditions to achieve the highest level of productivity with the smallest number of mistakes. These women had been chosen to be the subjects of the experiment.

They then began their experiments by raising the light levels in the production area. Within a couple of days, production went up and defects went down. The researchers were delighted with these results.

They then lowered the lighting levels to test the differences. But to their surprise, production levels went up again. They experimented with other working conditions. They raised and lowered the noise levels. They raised and lowered the room temperature. They altered the seating arrangements and the work order of the employees. But in every case, productivity levels went up. The researchers were baffled by these results.

Finally, they sat down with a focus group of the workers and explained to them what they had found. They asked them, "Why do you think it is that production levels have gone up, no matter what variables we changed in the working conditions?"

The answer they got back was surprising. The participants told the researchers that they had never before been singled out and treated as anything other than simple factory workers. When they were chosen to be subjects of this experiment, their levels of self-esteem and self-respect had gone up. They felt better about themselves. They felt more important. As a result, they did their work better than they had ever done it before. Each change in the working conditions reminded them that they had been specially selected for this study. They worked harder and better. And their productivity increased.

This breakthrough at the Hawthorne Electric Plant triggered the management revolution that has changed the world of work as we know it today. It was the discovery of the psychological factors of production that led to the breakthrough work of management researchers such as Maslow, McGregor, Herzberg, Drucker, and many others. Today, thousands of the best minds in the world are committed to improving the psychological factors that contribute to higher levels of productivity and output in every work situation.

Improvement Is Automatic

What psychologists and others have discovered is that the very act of observing a behavior tends to change that behavior for the better. This is one of the greatest breakthroughs in the understanding of personal performance. This critical discovery contains the key to dramatically improving the quality of any area of your life.

Sometimes I ask seminar audiences this question: "Imagine that there are several researchers from the local university in this room. Imagine also that these researchers will be observing you and writing a report later on how well you personally took notes during this seminar. Would that have any effect on your note-taking ability?"

Everyone smiles and agrees that if they knew that they were being carefully observed and evaluated on their note-taking ability, they would pay much more attention to the way they took notes. They would be much more aware, and they would do it far better than if no one was watching.

This point is simple yet profound and important. When you observe yourself engaging in any activity, you become more conscious and aware of that activity, and you do it better. When you pay attention to any element of your behavior, you tend to perform far better in that area than you would if you were not paying attention or if you had not thought about it at all.

The power of the Focal Point Process is that you learn how to identify the most vital actions and behaviors in each area, the ones that can bring you the greatest rewards and results in the shortest period of time. When you consciously focus on these areas, you will perform better and better. This process of continuous improvement will happen naturally and easily because you have put an "X" on the important behavior in advance.

The Law of Increasing Returns

To put it another way, the law of increasing returns applies to your use of the Focal Point Process, the reverse of the famous law of diminishing returns. The law of increasing returns says that the more you focus on doing the few things that represent the most valuable use of your time, the better you become at those activities and the less time it takes you to accomplish each one. Your returns on effort and energy increase. This is another key to doubling your income and doubling your time off.

The Efficiency Curve

The efficiency curve explains why some people earn several times as much as other people in the same field. It also

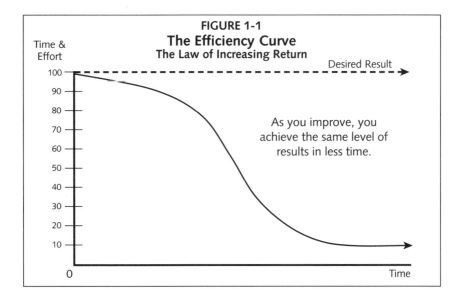

FIGURE 1-1
The Efficiency Curve
The Law of Increasing Return

Time & Effort

Desired Result

As you improve, you achieve the same level of results in less time.

Time

explains why some companies produce far more of a product or service at a consistently high level of quality and at a lower price than others. They can then pass their lower production costs onto their customers, sell for less, and undercut their competitors, thereby increasing their market share and their profits. This efficiency curve is the key to your success as well (see Figure 1-1).

This curve looks like a ski slope moving down from left to right. When you begin work on a new job or activity, usually you have to invest a good deal of time and effort to accomplish any results at all. This is the learning phase. But if you persist, eventually you will get better and better at that particular task. As you get better, you begin moving forward and downward along this curve, taking less and less time to get the same quality and quantity of results. Eventually, you reach the point where you can produce in one hour what a new person might take several hours to produce. Meanwhile, the quality of your work is equal to or greater than that of the less experienced person, who is spending many more hours to do the same job.

Your Habits Determine Your Destiny

Almost everything you do is determined by your habits. I would venture at least 95 percent. From the time you get up in the morning to the time you go to sleep at night, your habits largely control and dictate the words you say, the things you do, and the ways you react and respond. Successful, happy people have good habits that are life enhancing. Unsuccessful, unhappy people have habits that hurt them and hold them back.

Fortunately, all habits are both learned and learnable. You can learn any habit that you consider desirable or necessary if you are willing to work at it long enough and hard enough.

A habit can be defined as an automatic or conditioned response to stimuli. A habit, good or bad, is something you do naturally and easily, without thought or effort. Once developed, a habit takes on a momentum of its own, controlling your behavior and your responses to the events in your world. Once formed, a habit does not go away. It can only be replaced by a newer, better habit. We form our habits, and then our habits form us.

German philosopher Goethe once wrote, "Everything is hard before it is easy." You may need to exert tremendous discipline to develop new habits of thought and behavior. But once you have them firmly locked in, they enable you to accomplish vastly more, with less effort, than ever before.

Good habits are hard to develop but easy to live with; bad habits are easy to develop but hard to live with. The habits you have and the habits that have you will determine almost everything you achieve or fail to achieve.

Your job is to form good habits and make them your masters. Simultaneously, you must diligently work to eliminate your bad habits and free yourself from their negative consequences. Later, we will talk about how you can identify the habits that can help you the most and how you can most rapidly develop them.

The Grand Slam Formula

The Grand Slam Formula in the Focal Point Process is made up of four parts: simplification, leveraging, acceleration, and multiplication. The Grand Slam Formula is another key to doubling your income and doubling your time off.

Simplify

The first letter in *Slam* stands for *simplify*. To get better control of your time, to double your income and dramatically increase the quality of your personal life, you must learn to simplify everything you do. You must be continually reducing and eliminating activities that take up too much time and contribute very little to your goals.

You simplify your time and your life by stopping doing as many things of low value as possible. This will free more time to do the few things that really make a difference. To simplify your life, zero-based thinking is one of the most powerful strategies you can learn and apply on a regular basis.

Here's how it works. Ask yourself, "Is there anything I am doing right now that, knowing what I now know, I wouldn't get into again if I were starting over today?"

Is there any relationship, personal or business, that you wouldn't get into again today if you had it to do over? Is there any product, service, process, or expenditure of time or money in your work or business that, knowing what you now know, you wouldn't get into again today if you had it to do over?

If your answer is "yes," then your next question is, "How do I get out of this situation, and how fast?"

If you find yourself doing something that you would not start up again today, knowing what you now know, this activity is a prime candidate for downsizing or eliminating. Discontinuing just one major activity or separating yourself from one person who no longer belongs in your life can dramatically simplify your life, sometimes overnight.

Continually ask yourself whether there is anything you should do more of or less of, start doing, or stop doing altogether? These are questions you should ask and answer every day. They are important keys to simplification. Chapter Three deals exclusively and in detail with the simplification process.

Leverage

The second letter in the Grand Slam Formula stands for *leverage*. You use leverage to get the most out of yourself. You leverage your strengths and abilities to achieve more than you thought you could. The Greek philosopher Archimedes once said, "Give me a lever long enough and a place to stand, and I can move the world." This principle applies to you as well.

There are seven forms of leverage that you can develop. These forms of leverage are often available to you for the asking.

Other People's Knowledge

The first form of leverage is other people's knowledge. One key piece of knowledge applied to your situation can make an extraordinary difference in your results. It can save you an enormous amount of money and many hours, even weeks or months of hard work. For this reason, successful people are like radar screens, constantly sweeping the horizons of their lives, searching in books, magazines, tapes, articles, and conferences for ideas and insights they can use to help them to achieve their goals faster.

Other People's Energy

The second form of leverage is other people's energy. Highly effective people are always looking for ways to delegate and outsource lower-value activities so that they have more time to do the few things that give them the highest payoff. How can you use the energies of other people to help you to be more effective and productive?

Other People's Money

The third form of leverage is other people's money. Your ability to borrow and tap into the financial resources of other people can enable you to accomplish extraordinary things that would not be possible if you had to pay for them out of your own resources. You should always be looking for opportunities to borrow and invest money and achieve returns well beyond the cost of that money.

Other People's Successes

The fourth form of leverage is other people's successes. You can dramatically improve the quality of your results by study-

ing the successes enjoyed by other people and other companies. Successful people usually have paid a high price, in
money and emotion, difficulties and disappointment, to
achieve a particular goal. By studying their successes and learning from their experiences, you can often save yourself an
enormous amount of time and trouble.

Other People's Failures

The fifth form of leverage is other people's failures. Benjamin
Franklin once said, "Man can either buy his wisdom or borrow
it. By buying it, he pays full price in personal time and trea-
sure. But by borrowing it, he capitalizes on the lessons learned
from the failures of others."

Many of the greatest successes of history came about as the
result of carefully studying the failures of other people in the
same or similar fields and then learning from them. What or
who has failed in your field that you can learn from?

Other People's Ideas

A sixth form of leverage is other people's ideas. One good idea
is all you need to start a fortune. The more you read, learn, discuss, and experiment, the more likely it is that you will come
across an idea that, combined with your own abilities and
resources, will make you a great success in your field.

Other People's Contacts

The seventh form of leverage is other people's contacts or
other people's credibility. Each person you know knows many
other people, many of whom can be helpful to you. Whom do
you know who could open doors for you or introduce you to
the right people? Whom do you know who can help you to

achieve your goals faster? One introduction to one key person can change the entire direction of your life.

Accelerate

The third letter in the Grand Slam Formula stands for *accelerate*. Today, in our society, there is an incredible need for speed. Everyone is impatient. Everyone wants everything yesterday, even if they didn't know they wanted it until today. Anyone who can act quickly to satisfy the needs of other people can move rapidly to the front of the line. Always be looking for ways to do things faster for the key people and customers in your life.

Multiply

The fourth letter in *Slam* is *M*, which stands for *multiply*. The primary way you multiply yourself is by organizing and working with other people who have skills and abilities that are complementary to your own. A good manager becomes a multiplication sign in that he or she coordinates the work of different people so that the outcome of the team is far greater than the total outcome of the individuals working alone. The effective manager creates a high-performance climate that elicits extraordinary performance from ordinary people. Your ability to assemble a team of excellent people and then help your team accomplish important tasks is central to your long-term success. It is the key to multiplying yourself and your abilities.

Double Your Time Off

To double your time off, you need the power of decisiveness more than any other single quality or attribute. Your ability to decide to take time off and then to stick to your decision is the key to doubling your time off and spending more time in your personal relationships.

Many people are convinced that they have so much to do that they have no real choice about whether they can take time off. They often feel that they have to sacrifice their personal lives for their work. But this is seldom true.

It would not be an exaggeration to assert that as much as 80 percent of a person's time at work is spent in activities that contribute very little to the work the person is being paid to do. Half of the average person's working time is simply wasted. It is consumed in idle socializing with coworkers, personal telephone calls, and personal business. It is eaten up by arriving late and leaving early and by taking extended coffee and lunch breaks.

Hard time drives out soft time. In other words, if you waste time at work by socializing or engaging in low-value activities, the work itself does not go away. The work remains. It still has to be done. As it is delayed and left undone, it begins to build up like an avalanche overhang. The undone work begins to crowd out nonwork activities. This hard time of essential work eventually drives out the soft time of home life and recreation.

Consider the story of the little girl who goes to her mother and asks, "Mommy, why does daddy bring home a briefcase full of work every night and work all evening and never spend any time with us?"

Mommy replies, "Honey, you have to understand. Daddy can't get all his work done at the office during the day. That's why he has to bring it home and work on it in the evening."

The little girl looks up at her mommy and says, "Why don't they just put him in a slower class?"

Most people who are not taking enough time for their families and their personal activities have fallen into the bad habit of working inefficiently and ineffectively during the work day. They get less and less done in more and more time. They socialize with their coworkers, and they work on low-value tasks. Meanwhile, the critical jobs on which their success depends build up, causing them enormous stress and giving them the feeling of being harried and overworked.

One advantage highly productive people have over average people is that they have learned how to think and act more effectively than others do. And whatever anyone else has done or is doing, you can do as well, with practice.

Six Steps to Doubling Your Income and Doubling Your Time Off

1. Identify the few tasks that contribute the greatest value to your work. Think your work through carefully. Discuss it with your boss and your coworkers. Identify your key tasks with absolute clarity so that you know without a shadow of a doubt what you can do to make the greatest contribution.

2. Identify the routine tasks and activities that consume so much time but contribute little or nothing to your long-term goals at work. Begin today to delegate those tasks to others, one at a time. Eliminate them altogether wherever possible. Outsource anything that can be done by any other person or company. Reduce the amount of time you spend in low-value, time-consuming activities. Be adamant about discontinuing tasks and activities that are of little importance.

3. Use the Grand Slam Formula to dramatically increase your output and your results. Simplify, leverage, accelerate, and multiply your talents and abilities through others.

4. Decide today to take at least one full day each week off work during which you spend time exclusively on your personal pursuits. During this time off, refuse to do anything associated with work. Do not read, make telephone calls, catch up on your correspondence, work on your computer, or do anything else work related. Let your brain completely recharge and rejuvenate by turning your attention to something apart from the work you do during the week.

5. Once you are comfortable taking one day off each week, expand your time off to two days, a full weekend, every week. Begin to schedule a three-day vacation every three months and eventually every two months. Begin to schedule two to four weeks of vacation every year. Reorganize your life so that time off becomes a major priority.

The more you get your time and your life under control, the more you will get done and the more enjoyable your work will be. The more you get done, the more free time you will have. The more free time you have, the more rested you will be. The more rested you are, the more alert and productive you will be when you are working, thereby getting even more done.

6. Start today to pay closer attention to the things you do. Be more conscious and aware of yourself and your actions. Think about your tasks carefully before you begin. Identify your most important tasks and concentrate on them single-mindedly. The very act of continually thinking through your activities before you begin will develop within you new habits of thought and action that will lead to greater levels of productivity and performance. You will be amazed at the improvements that take place in every part of your life, and they will take place far faster than you can imagine.

CHAPTER TWO

Double Your Productivity

The first requisite of success is the ability to apply your physical and mental energies to one problem without growing weary.
—THOMAS EDISON

The Focal Point Process shows you how to double your income and double your time off simultaneously. Both are desirable and necessary. And achieving both is not only possible but also amazingly simple if you know how. Both are achievable when you change your thinking and do more of the right things in your work and your personal life.

The formula you need to double your productivity is easy to explain, but it takes effort and determination to implement. It is simply this: Perform more and more tasks of higher value and delegate, delay, outsource, and eliminate tasks of lower value.

The starting point is to think through your work before you begin. Your first responsibility, the primary job of a knowledge worker, is to determine what is to be done. The more accurate you can be about the "what," the more productive you can be when you begin on the "how" and "when."

Five Questions for Superior Performance

There are five questions you must ask yourself regularly if you want to perform at your very best:

1. *What am I trying to do?* Define the ideal goal or outcome you are striving for before you begin. If you are working with others, make sure everybody is crystal clear about the desired result before anyone starts work.

2. *How am I trying to do it?* Make sure that this is the best way. Ask whether there could be another way. Always remain open to the possibility that you could be wrong. Think through and analyze your approach to be sure that it is the very best way to approach your goal or objective.

3. *What are my assumptions?* Are you making any assumptions with regard to the market, the actions or performance of other people, the underlying motives of the key players, or the outcome of future events? Remember, as time management expert Alec Mackenzie wrote, "Errant assumptions lie at the root of most failures."

4. *What if my assumptions were wrong?* What if something that you believed to be true turned out not to be true at all? Perhaps someone you are negotiating with is only using this negotiation with you to get a better price or deal from someone else. Always be willing to question your most cherished assumptions.

5. *What would I have to do differently if my key assumptions were wrong?* What would you do if this approach failed completely? What are your alternatives? If you were not doing it this way, would you start it over again? Always be willing to ask, "How else could I go about achieving this same result?"

Clarity Is the Key

Clarity is everything. To perform at your very best and double your productivity, you must be absolutely clear about what you want to accomplish. You must then identify and pursue the best way to achieve it. You must be open to new information, willing to accept feedback and self-correct, and willing to abandon one way of working and embrace another if the circumstances warrant it. And you must be fast on your feet.

According to reports generated from the Menninger Institute in Kansas City, flexibility is the most important single quality you can develop to survive and thrive in the twenty-first century. Flexibility entails openness, receptivity, and the willingness to try new methods and techniques. Flexibility means that you practice zero-based thinking continually.

One way to become more flexible is to get your ego out of the way. Detach yourself from the situation. Be more concerned with *what's* right rather than with *who's* right. Your only question should be, "Does it work?"

Whenever you encounter resistance or stress in pursuing a particular course of action, stand back and question your methods. Ask, "How else could we approach this?" Be open to all possibilities, including abandoning the goal or project altogether.

Increase Your Productivity

The starting point of higher productivity is clear goals. For a goal to be effective in guiding behavior, it must be specific and measurable. It must be believable and achievable. It must be written out and time bounded. The greater clarity you have with regard to your goals, the more you will get done and the faster you will accomplish what you do.

The second key to high productivity is clear, written plans of action. Every minute you spend in planning will save you as many as ten minutes in execution.

Make a list of every single step of the task, or of your day, before you begin. Always work from a list. Think on paper. Working from a list keeps you on track and gives you a visual record of accomplishment. The very act of writing out a list and referring to it constantly should increase your productivity by at least 25 percent from the time you start doing it.

Third, set priorities on your list. Think the list through before you begin the first task. Use the 80/20 Rule continually. Identify the 20 percent of activities on your list that can account for 80 percent of the value of your entire list. Begin your work on the items in the top 20 percent before you do anything else.

The most important measure of the importance or value of any task is the potential consequences of doing it or failing to do it. An important task or activity has significant consequences. An unimportant task has few or no consequences at all.

Completing a critical assignment for your boss or for a major customer is a top priority because the consequences of failing to do it can be significant. Having lunch with a coworker is an activity of low value because the consequences of doing it or not doing it are insignificant.

Use the ABCDE Method Daily

Use the ABCDE Method to set work priorities. Place one of these letters before each task on your list before you begin.

■ An "A" task is something that is important. It is something you *must* do. It is something for which there are significant consequences if you do it or fail to do it. If you have more than one "A" task to do, organize them as A-1, A-2, A-3, and so on, in order of importance.

■ A "B" task is something that you *should* do. There are consequences if it is done or not done, but it is not as important as an "A" task. Never work on a "B" task when there is an "A" task left undone. Refuse to work on a lower priority when there is a higher priority waiting.

■ A "C" task is something that would be *nice* to do but has no consequences at all. For example, reading the paper, going for coffee with a coworker, or calling home to see what's for dinner are all "C" tasks. They contribute nothing to your job or your success. Never work on a "C" task when there is a "B" task left undone.

■ A "D" task is anything you can delegate to someone else. The rule is that you should delegate everything that can possibly be done by anyone else so that you can free more time to do the few things only you can do.

Ask yourself, "What can I and only I do that, if done well, will make a real difference to my company?" Delegate as much as possible so that you can spend more time working on the one task that is the answer to this question, the one task that can really make a difference.

■ An "E" task is something you can *eliminate* altogether. Doing it or not doing it has no consequences at all. It is something that may have been important in the past but that you can discontinue today with no real effect on your job or your future.

Separate the Urgent From the Important

Another way to set priorities before you begin is to separate the urgent from the important. An urgent task is something that seems pressing or timely, such as a phone call or an emergency. An important task is something that can have serious consequences if it is done or not done (see Figure 2-1).

■ Something that is both urgent and important is a task that is "in your face." This is something you have to do immediately. Your job may depend on it. The consequences for nonperformance of an urgent and important task can be serious. This type of task is always associated with external demands and other people. This type of work, urgent and important, is where most people spend their time.

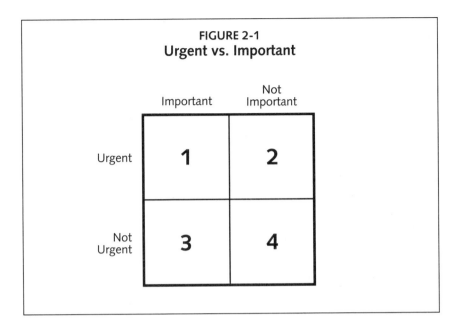

FIGURE 2-1
Urgent vs. Important

■ Tasks that are important but not urgent are usually tasks on which you can procrastinate at least temporarily. These are also the tasks that can have the greatest possible consequences, positive or negative, for the long term.

For example, writing a key report, pursuing a course of study, spending time with your children when they are growing up, and even exercising to keep fit are all tasks that are important but not urgent. You can put them off until later, and you often do. But they can have significant positive or negative consequences in the long term.

These tasks and activities can give you tremendous leverage and enable you to multiply yourself and your efforts. The more time you spend on tasks that are important though not urgent, the more effective and productive you become in the long term.

■ Tasks that are urgent but not important include ringing telephones, coworkers who want to talk to you, and incoming mail. These tasks appear pressing, but in terms of consequences they are not important at all. Most people spend an enormous amount of time doing things that are urgent but not important. While appearing busy, they often delude themselves into thinking that they are doing something of value, even though this is seldom true.

■ Tasks that are neither important nor urgent are largely a waste of time, especially when they take you away from more productive activities. Many people spend half their time doing things that are neither important nor urgent. They make the mistake of thinking that they are doing something of value just because they are at work when they are doing it.

A major key to high productivity is for you to focus on completing all your urgent and important work and then to concentrate on activities that are important but not urgent. Meanwhile, you must delay, defer, delegate, and discontinue all other tasks. You must discipline yourself to stop doing the things that are urgent but not important and those that are neither urgent nor important.

Three Questions for High Productivity

1. Keep asking yourself, "What are my highest-value activities?" What are the things you do that contribute the greatest value to your work?

2. Ask yourself, "Why am I on the payroll?" What exactly have you been hired to accomplish in terms of measurable results?

3. And keep asking, "What is the most valuable use of my time right now?" This is the key question in time and personal management. You should ask and answer this question every hour of every day. Whatever your answer, you should be working on this task most of the time, if not all the time.

Once you have thought through your work and decided on your most valuable task, you must discipline yourself to start it immediately and stay with it until it is complete.

When you concentrate single-mindedly on a single task, without diversion or distraction, you get it done far faster than if you start and stop and then come back to the task and pick it up again. You can reduce the amount of time you spend on a major task by as much as 80 percent simply by refusing to do anything else until that task is complete.

Seven Keys to Higher Productivity

There are seven additional ways to increase your productivity, performance, and output, either alone or in combination with others.

1. *Work harder at what you do.* When you work, work all the time you work. Don't waste time. Don't look at the workplace as a place to socialize with your friends. Instead, when you come to work, put your head down and work full blast for the entire day. This practice alone will enable you to double your productivity.

2. *Work faster.* Develop a sense of urgency. Get on with the job. Don't waste time. Develop and maintain a fast tempo in your work activities. Deliberately move faster from task to

task. You'll be amazed at how much more you'll get done just by deciding to pick up the pace in everything you do.

3. *Work on higher-value activities.* Remember that the number of hours you work is not nearly as important as the value of the tasks you complete, the quality and quantity of results you achieve. The more time you spend on higher-value tasks, the greater results you will obtain from every hour you put in.

4. *Do things you are better at.* When you work on tasks at which you are especially skilled and experienced, you can accomplish much more in a shorter period of time than could an inexperienced person. In addition, work at getting *better* at the most important things you do. Nothing will increase the quality and quantity of your output faster than becoming excellent at performing the most important tasks that are expected of you.

5. *Bunch your tasks.* Do several similar activities all at the same time. By writing all your letters, filling out all your expense reports, or preparing all your proposals at the same time, you get better and faster with each task. You move more quickly along the learning curve. Each subsequent task takes you less time. You can reduce the amount of time it takes to perform a particular task by up to 80 percent by doing several similar tasks one after the other.

6. *Simplify your work* so that it is easier to do. Consolidate several parts of the job into a single task so that there are fewer steps. Eliminate lower-value activities altogether.

7. *Work longer hours.* Notwithstanding my points elsewhere regarding time off from work, it is true that if you start a little earlier and stay a little later, you will be more productive.

By starting your day earlier than the average person, you beat the traffic into work. By staying a little later, you leave after the traffic. By doing both, you can add two or three hours to your productive working day without really affecting your lifestyle. These extra hours are all you need to become one of the most productive and highest-paid people in your field.

The Race Is On

Compete against yourself to see how much you can get done of high value each day. Make it a game. Set schedules and deadlines for yourself and race against the deadlines. See whether you can get more and more done in less and less time.

Develop a clear vision for yourself as a highly productive person. Think about the times in your life when you were most productive, effective, and efficient. Think about situations in which you were doing the right things in the right way. You were getting a lot done in a short period of time. You felt terrific about yourself and your performance. You were in that magical state of flow, and you felt happy and exhilarated.

Project forward five years and imagine that you are now one of the most productive people in your field. What would you look like? How would you be working? What would you be working on? What would be your guiding principles for personal performance? How would people describe you to others in terms of the way you work? Let your vision of the future guide your present performance.

Once you have a clear vision of your ideal future, put an "X" on the specific image of yourself that you like the most. Continually visualize and see yourself as if you were already that person. Remember, the person you see is the person you will be. Hold that image in your mind until you become that person in your reality.

With your ideal vision clear, set specific goals for yourself in terms of your work life. Imagine that you have the ability to produce any quality or quantity of work that you desire. What would it be? What are your specific goals and objectives for your work and your personal life?

Motivation includes motive. You must be clear about why you are doing what you are doing. Why do you work as hard as you do? What do you really want to accomplish? What is the fastest and most direct way to get from where you are to where you want to go?

What additional knowledge and skills will you need to double your productivity and perform at your best? Become an expert at time management. Read the books, listen to the audio programs, and practice, practice, practice until you are one of the most productive people in your business.

What habits and behaviors would be most helpful for you to develop to increase your productivity? Concentrate on developing the habits of result orientation, focus, concentration, discipline, and persistence. These become internal motivators and drivers for high performance.

My favorite organizing principle for high productivity is single handling, in which you concentrate single-mindedly on one thing, the most important thing, all day long. Once you have programmed this work habit into yourself, you'll be amazed at how much you get done.

The daily habits of planning, setting priorities, and then starting with your highest-value task will do more to help you than perhaps anything else in time management. You can develop these habits by practicing them over and over again until they become automatic.

What daily activities should you practice to ensure that you perform at your very best? Keep a checklist of time management principles and review it regularly. Make sure that you are always working on the highest-value use of your time.

Finally, what one action commitment are you going to make as a result of what you have just learned? What specific action are you going to take to increase your productivity, performance, and output? Whatever it is, do it now!

Toward a Philosophy of Time

Time management is really life management, personal management, management of yourself. People who value themselves highly allocate their time carefully. They give their time usage a lot of thought. When you love your life, you love every minute of it. You are very careful about misusing or wasting any of the precious minutes and hours of each day.

Effective people plan their time in tight time segments. They think in terms of ten- and fifteen-minute blocks. They plan every day in detail, in advance. They make every minute count. As a result, they accomplish vastly more than the average person, and they feel much better about themselves.

When you begin to manage your time and your life more carefully, you begin to place a higher value on every minute and every hour. You begin to place a higher value on yourself and your life as well. The better you manage your time, the more you like and respect yourself. And the more you like and respect yourself, the better you manage your time. Each reinforces the other.

The law of increasing returns is your friend. The more you use and practice these time management principles, the better and more easily they will work for you. You will get more and better results. You will see continual improvements in your effectiveness and your output. In a few days or weeks, you will be astonished at how much more productive you are.

CHAPTER THREE

Simplify Your Life

It is a simple task to make things complex, but a complex task to make them simple.

—MEYER'S LAW

T his is a wonderful time to be alive. The incredible rate of change we are experiencing is creating more opportunities and possibilities for us than ever. You have more options in more areas than you have ever had before, and the number of options available to you is increasing every day and every month.

At the same time, you are overwhelmed with more tasks and more responsibilities than you ever had before. You are swamped with jobs that you need to get done, books and magazines you need to read, people you need to get back to, projects you need to start or complete, and goals you want to accomplish. And like a nonstop production line, the jobs keep coming, one after the other, far too fast for you to ever get on top of them all.

You are caught in a dilemma. You want to fulfill your potential and achieve everything that is possible for you at work. You want to earn the greatest amount of money in the shortest period of time. You want to be a great success in your career. But at the same time, you do not want to sacrifice your family life, your relationships, your health, or the personal activities that are so important to you.

You want to have it all. You want far greater accomplishment on one hand and far more balance and simplicity on the other hand.

The good news is that thousands of successful, happy men and women have discovered methods, techniques, and strategies that make all these things possible. And whatever others have done, within reason, you can do as well.

A single mother in my Advanced Coaching Program was earning just over $30,000 a year when she began applying the principles covered here to her work and her life. She was working seventy to eighty hours per week and was completely overwhelmed with her need to be successful in her career and simultaneously spend sufficient time with her daughter.

Within five years, she increased her income to more than $300,000 a year and reduced her work week to thirty-eight hours. Her formula was simple. She dedicated herself to getting better and better at the two or three activities that contributed the most value to her work. She delegated, outsourced, and eliminated everything else. Today she performs far fewer tasks, but the value of those tasks is ten times greater than the total output of her work a few years ago.

The starting point of simplification is for you to reduce the number of things you do in your work and in your personal life. You can control your time only to the degree to which you discontinue tasks that are of little value to you. You must stop doing some of the things that you have become accustomed to doing over the years. You may even have to stop doing some things that you do well and you enjoy.

As the result of many years of study and practice, I developed what I call the "law of complexity." When you apply this law of complexity to time management and simplification, you will immediately simplify your life, increase your output, and start getting more enjoyment from everything you do.

The law of complexity says that the level of complexity of any task is equal to the square of the number of different steps in that task. Complexity can be defined as the potential for increased costs, increased time, or increased mistakes.

For example, a simple task is something you do yourself. If you decide to make a personal telephone call, there is only one step. The task has a complexity factor of one; one squared is the same as one times one, so the complexity level of a simple, individual task is one. You pick up the phone, you make the call, and you put the phone down.

However, if you ask someone else to make a phone call for you, you have added a step to the process. Your complexity level increases to two squared, or four.

This means that the potential increase in time, cost, and mistakes or misunderstandings has increased from one (a single step) to four (two steps), a huge leap in the potential for increased time, cost, and mistakes.

Furthermore, suppose you ask someone else to ask a third party to make the telephone call for you. Now you have three steps. This gives you a complexity level of three squared, or nine.

The possibility of increased time, increased expense, and increased misunderstandings or mistakes has now jumped from a complexity level of one if you made the call yourself to a complexity level of nine if you have someone else ask someone else to make the call.

An activity with four steps has a complexity level of four squared, or sixteen. This greatly increases the potential for increased cost, time, and complexity. A task with five steps has a complexity level of five squared, or twenty-five. A task with ten steps has a complexity level of ten squared, or 100.

What this means is that the level of complexity increases exponentially as the number of steps increases arithmetically. The level of complexity also declines exponentially as you eliminate steps from the process (see Figure 3-1).

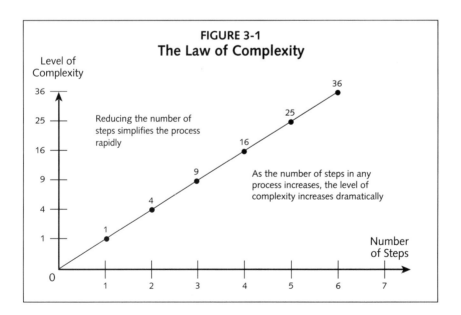

FIGURE 3-1
The Law of Complexity

Level of Complexity

Reducing the number of steps simplifies the process rapidly

As the number of steps in any process increases, the level of complexity increases dramatically

Number of Steps

This law of complexity suggests how you can dramatically simplify your life by continually looking for ways to reduce the number of steps necessary to complete any task.

A major life insurance company had a problem. When the company received an application for life insurance from the field, it took six weeks to issue an approval or disapproval of the policy. By that time, the prospective client had often lost interest or gone somewhere else.

The insurance company brought in a consultant who applied the complexity theory to the approval process of a life insurance application. He found that the application form passed through twenty-two different hands. Each person checked and approved a particular part of the policy before it arrived on the desk of the final decision-maker. The entire process took six weeks. However, the actual amount of time spent on the policy turned out to be less than an hour.

With this information in hand, the insurance company dramatically simplified the process. They assigned the first twenty-one steps to a single person. The second person merely double-checked the work of the first person. As a result, they reduced the turnaround time for approvals from six weeks to twenty-four hours. Their insurance underwriting business increased by more than a billion dollars as a result.

The residential mortgage department of Citibank of New York did much the same thing. Previously, from the time it received a mortgage application, because of the number of steps required for approval, it took five to six weeks to decide whether to fund the mortgage. By that time, the potential home buyer often had gone elsewhere.

By reducing the number of steps in the approval process, Citibank reduced the turnaround time from six weeks to twenty-four hours. As a result of this incredible speed, it became the mortgage lender of choice among financial institutions and increased its mortgage portfolio by hundreds of millions of dollars with no decline in quality.

The Seven *R*s of Simplification

Use one or more of these steps to simplify and streamline every area of your personal and work life.

■ **The first *R* is *rethinking*.** Whenever you find yourself overwhelmed with too much to do and too little time, stop and think about your work. Stand back and ask yourself, "Could there be a better way?"

Especially when you face resistance, stress, or difficulties of any kind, stop pushing and driving. Instead, put yourself in the position of an outside consultant. Imagine that you have been brought in to evaluate your own situation and give yourself objective advice on how to handle it. Remain open and receptive. Be willing to consider the possibility that your current approach is wrong.

■ **The second *R* is *reevaluating*.** When you get new information, stop the clock, like calling a time out in a football game, and reevaluate your situation based on the way it is today. Jack Welch, president of General Electric, calls this the "reality principle."

The reality principle requires that you be absolutely honest with yourself and deal with the situation based on the way it really is today, right now, not the way you wish it were or the way it might have been in the past.

Jack Welch begins every discussion or evaluation of a problem with the question, "What's the reality?" You should do this as well. In *The Devil's Dictionary*, Ambrose Bierce wrote, "Fanaticism is redoubling your efforts after your aim has been forgotten." Don't let this happen to you.

■ **The third *R* is *reorganizing*.** The purpose of reorganizing your life or work is to ensure a greater level of outputs from the same quantity and quality of inputs. In times of rapid change and turbulence, you must reorganize continually. As one high-tech executive said recently, "In this business, you have to throw out all your assumptions every three weeks."

Be prepared to reorganize your workspace. Be prepared to reorganize your schedule throughout the day. Be prepared to reorganize your order and priority of activities. Be open to the possibility that there is always a better way to do the job than the way you are currently working. Keep searching for that better way.

■ **The fourth *R* is *restructuring*.** In restructuring you channel more of your time, energy, money, and resources into the top 20 percent of activities that generate the most revenues and the greatest profits. Companies restructure by focusing more of their resources on the products, services, and activities that customers value the most highly. Simultaneously, they delegate, outsource, and eliminate non–revenue-generating activities that customers don't care about.

When you restructure your own activities, you continually focus and refocus your time and energy on the few things you do that account for most of your results. You concentrate single-mindedly on your most valuable tasks.

■ *Reengineering* **is the fifth key to simplification.** This is one of the most powerful practices for simplifying your work and your personal life. In reengineering, your entire focus is on process improvement. You constantly look for newer, better, faster, cheaper, and easier ways to accomplish the task and achieve the desired result.

You begin reengineering your work by making a list of all the steps in a particular work process, from start to finish. You then set a goal to reduce the number of steps on the list by 30 percent the first time through. You will be amazed at how easy it is to accomplish this task the first time you do it.

Six Ways to Reengineer Your Life and Work

- *Consolidate* several tasks into one single task.
- *Assign several tasks* to a single person rather than having them spread out among several people. This is called job compression by responsibility expansion.
- *Outsource* particular tasks and have them done by other companies or individuals who specialize in that area.
- *Delegate* tasks to other people or other departments.
- *Eliminate* certain tasks altogether by determining that they are no longer necessary or essential to the finished product.
- *Change the order* in which tasks are done to reduce bottlenecks and increase efficiency.

Continually review any complex task consisting of several steps and look for ways to reengineer it, simplifying it so that you can get it done faster and more efficiently than before.

■ **The sixth *R* in simplification is *reinventing*.** Here, you re-create yourself completely. In times of rapid change, you should be reinventing yourself and your job every six to twelve months. Practice zero-based thinking continually. Keep asking yourself, "If I were not doing it this way, knowing what I now know, would I start it up again this way?"

Imagine that you are starting your job or your career over again. Is there anything you would do more of? Is there anything you would do less of? Is there anything you would start doing that you are not doing today? Is there anything you would stop doing altogether?

You are going to have a variety of different jobs and positions throughout your life. Keep looking ahead and thinking about what you might like to do. Ask yourself, "What is my next job going to be?" What would you like it to be?

Then ask yourself, "What is my next career going to be?" What would you like it to be? If you do not ask and answer these questions for yourself, someone else may come along and answer them for you.

■ **The seventh *R* in simplification is *regaining control*.** In this step, you set new goals and create new plans. You make new decisions and commit yourself to new actions. You accept complete responsibility and take charge of your life. You don't wait for good things to happen to you. You go out and make them happen. You take charge of your time and your life.

Identify Your Values

In the Focal Point Process, determining your values is the first step to simplifying your life. What is important to you? What values or unifying principles do you care about the most with regard to your personal life?

Some things you might value could be peace, simplicity, tranquility, contentment, satisfaction, happiness, love, and joy. Select the five values that are most important to you and organize them by priority (see the Appendix).

Create Your Ideal Future Vision

Based on your values, create a vision for yourself as if your life was ideal in every way sometime in the future. Imagine that you have no limitations. Imagine that you could design your ideal lifestyle and your ideal calendar. What would they look like?

Determine Your Goals

With your values and your vision clear, you then set specific goals to simplify your life. Your ability to choose between alternatives and then to make firm decisions is the most powerful tool you have to achieve anything you really want. If for any reason you are not happy with your current situation, you can make new choices and decisions about exactly what you want and then go to work to make that a reality.

Practice "idealization" at all times. Think back to the happiest times in your personal life and the most organized and productive times in your work life and imagine how you could re-create those times in your future.

Ask yourself, "If I had only six months to live, how would I change my life?"

If you only had a short time left on Earth, what would you do more of or less of? What would you start doing or stop doing? What would you get into or get out of? How would you spend your time, and whom would you spend it with?

If you were financially independent today, what activities in your life would you discontinue altogether? What steps could you take immediately to simplify your life and increase your levels of peace and happiness?

What is your focal point with regard to your values, vision, and goals? Where should you put the "X" in your work or personal life to get the greatest immediate impact? What should you do, or stop doing, immediately?

Learn How to Say No

What habits or behaviors should you practice to simplify your life and keep it simplified? Perhaps the very best habit you can develop is the habit of saying "no" to any demand on your time that is not consistent with what you want most in life.

The word "no" is one of the most powerful words you will ever learn. Just say "no" to any demand or request that is not a high-value use of your time. Then you can say "yes" to the activities you really enjoy.

Six Ways to Simplify Your Daily Life

Begin today to simplify your work and your personal life. Set it as a goal, make a plan, and work on simplification every day. Here are some ways to get started.

1. Clean up the clutter in your life. Clear off your workspace completely before you begin work. Even if you have to put things on the floor, you should only have one task on the desk in front of you at any one time.

2. Go through your stacks of reading material with a garbage bag and begin throwing things away. Much of it no longer has value. Any magazine that is more than six months old is junk. Any information you can get somewhere else is junk. Most materials put aside for filing or storage are never looked at again. There are warehouses full of dead files that eventually have to be thrown away. There are homes, offices, and desks with piles of materials that will never be looked at by human eyes again.

3. To increase breathing space in your life, try leaving things off. Resist the temptation to turn on the radio at home or in your car. Leave the television off when you get up or arrive home. Create periods of silence in your life so that your mind can relax and function better.

One great advantage of leaving things off is that you will find yourself spending more time talking openly and honestly with your family and friends. As soon as you turn on the television or radio, all communication grinds to a halt. You can dramatically improve the quality of your life simply by developing the habit of leaving things off.

Many people have gotten rid of their television sets completely or moved them to a separate room. They are astonished at the improvement that takes place in the quality of their personal lives as a result.

4. Go through your car, your closets, and your garage and get rid of everything that is out of fashion, obsolete, unnecessary, or irreparable. Break yourself of the "pack rat" mentality so many people learned from their parents. Give things away to needy people and needy causes. Keep your life clean and simple, refined and elegant.

5. Practice solitude on a daily basis. Take thirty to sixty minutes each day and sit quietly by yourself. Allow your mind to relax. Breathe deeply and let your mind float, wandering from subject to subject, with no pressure or direction.

The daily practice of solitude can change your life. Every person who has ever accepted this advice and begun practicing solitude has been astonished at the overall improvement of the quality of his or her life. Sometimes, in solitude, you will come up with ideas and insights that are so profound and powerful that they change the entire direction of your career or your personal life. Just try it a couple of times and see.

6. Make a specific action commitment based on what you have learned in this chapter. Do something. Do anything. But take action immediately to begin to simplify your life. Once you have taken the first action, you will find yourself automatically propelled into taking action after action. In no time at all, you will have your life completely under control.

CHAPTER FOUR

Tap Your Most Precious Resource

Success is focusing the full power of all you are on what you have a burning desire to achieve.

—WILFERD A. PETERSON

Your ability to think is your most precious resource. Your ability to decide and then take action determines everything that happens to you. And your ability to choose your own thoughts and reactions is the one thing over which you have complete control.

Bob Silver was a thirty-two-year-old man living in Chicago, Illinois. A year after he attended one of my seminars, he got in touch with me and told me a remarkable story about how his life had changed over the previous twelve months.

Before he began, he was overweight, was between jobs, had been married and divorced twice, and was deeply in debt. He was extremely negative and was generally angry with everyone he felt was part of "the system." He was convinced that the cards were stacked against him. Life was unfair. He saw himself as very much a victim of a string of bad luck. He believed that all his problems, and the problems of society at large, were the fault of people who seemed to be doing much better than he was.

He came to my seminar reluctantly on a free ticket given to him by a friend who insisted that he come. He sat there with his arms folded, his chin down, largely impervious to this "motivational stuff," which he *knew* was both untrue and useless.

In his letter, he wrote and told me that something that I said went off in his head like a thunderclap, bringing him bolt upright and changing his thinking completely. It was when I said, "You are where you are and what you are because of yourself, nothing else. Nature is neutral. Nature doesn't care. If you do what other successful people do, you will enjoy the same results and rewards that they do. And if you don't, you won't."

You have probably heard this thought expressed many times in many ways. For him, it was a life-changing event. He realized in a single flash that deep down in his heart, he really wanted to be happy and successful. He wanted to be valued and respected by others. He also saw clearly, for the first time, that because of his attitude, he was unwittingly sabotaging himself in every situation he got into.

He walked out of that seminar determined to change his thinking and his behavior. One year later, he had turned his life around. He had a good job and had been promoted twice. He had lost thirty pounds. He was happily remarried and living in a new apartment. He felt terrific about himself and looked forward to every day, both at home and at work. He was a new man.

What had happened? He had learned the great truth that has been discovered and rediscovered throughout history: Your most precious resource is your mind. Your ability to think, plan, decide, and take action is the most powerful force for good in your life. This power is the starting point of every good thing that happens to you. When you take full control over your thinking, your entire world changes.

We have now entered what Harlow Shapley of Harvard University calls the Psychozoic Age, or the Age of the Mind. Your mind is so powerful that, properly directed, it can bring you almost anything you want in life. You have within you, right now, untapped reservoirs of potential so great that in your entire life, you will never be able to do even a small fraction of what you are truly capable of doing.

The Turning Point

I started out in life with few advantages, working at laboring jobs, unemployed for as much as five months of every year. I had a limited education, no experience, and few contacts. One day, I began asking, "Why are some people more successful than others?"

My search for the answer to this question has dominated and directed my life since I was nineteen years old. My first great discovery was the Aristotelian principle of causality. Today, we call it the law of cause and effect. In biblical terms, it is the law of sowing and reaping. Sir Isaac Newton called it the law of action and reaction. This is the great law of Western civilization. It underlies more than 2,000 years of advances in science, medicine, technology, and business.

The law of cause and effect says that for every effect there is a specific cause or causes. This law says that everything happens for a reason. It says that success, business or personal, is not an accident. Failure is not an accident. Both have specific cause-and-effect relationships that explain them.

In its simplest form, the law of cause and effect says that if there is an effect in your life that you want, you merely have to trace that effect back and find someone who at one time did not have that effect. You find out what that person did to achieve the effect you desire. You then do the same things he or she did. If you do the same things other successful people do, eventually you will get the same results they do. It is no miracle. It is a matter of law.

This discovery exploded in my mind when I was twenty-three years old, just as it exploded in the mind of Bob Silver in Chicago. Just imagine! You can be, have, or do anything you want in life if you simply find out how other people achieved it before you and then do the same things yourself. Whether you are tall or short, young or old, black or white, male or female, educated or uneducated, new immigrant or a descendant of the Puritans, if you do what other successful people do, you'll eventually get the same results they are getting. It is entirely up to you.

Philosopher Bertrand Russell wrote, "The very best proof that something can be done is the fact that others have already done it."

Abraham Lincoln wrote, "That some have succeeded greatly is proof that others can as well."

Open-mindedness and the willingness to revise your thinking in the face of new information can give you tremendous advantages for succeeding in a world of rapid change. When I learned this law, I did not question it. I simply accepted it as true and aggressively applied it to everything I attempted.

Putting the Principle Into Practice

When I got into sales, I searched out and applied every bit of information on sales methods and techniques that I could learn from other successful salespeople. And they worked. In no time at all, I was among the top salespeople in my organization.

When I got into sales management, I learned everything I could about managing salespeople. Within a year, I had ninety-five salespeople working for me, each of whom I had recruited and trained personally.

When I went into real estate development, I read more than twenty books on the subject, including how to locate property, how to arrange financing, and how to develop, lease, and sell a piece of real estate. Over the next five years, I bought, sold, developed, leased, and subdivided more than $50 million of industrial, commercial, and residential property.

Often when I explain this cause-and-effect principle, people dismiss it as being too simplistic to apply to their own situations, but the most powerful principles are almost always the simplest. That is why greater success and achievement are possible for almost everyone.

Here was my big breakthrough. I learned that the most important application of the law of cause and effect is this: *Thoughts are causes and conditions are effects.*

Put another way, thought is creative. Your thoughts are the causes that create the conditions of your life. Everything you have in your life today you have attracted to yourself by the way you think. You can change your life because you can change the way you think. The reason some people are more successful than others is simple. Successful people think differently from unsuccessful people. And if you develop the ways of thinking of successful people, you will soon enjoy the results successful people enjoy.

The Greatest Discovery

The most powerful application of the law of cause and effect is this: *You become what you think about most of the time.*

What an idea this is! Some of the greatest minds in history have stood in awe at the power of this great thought: You become what you think about most of the time.

In the movie *Firefox,* starring Clint Eastwood, the plot revolves around a new Russian fighter and bomber jet so advanced that it was controlled by the pilot's mind. The pilot's thoughts determined the direction and performance of the airplane, traveling at tremendous speeds. Clint Eastwood's character was fluent in English and Russian. As he escaped with the plane, he had to remind himself to think in Russian, the way the plane had been programmed.

Your mind is the same. The direction of your life and everything that happens to you is determined by the way you think, by the thoughts going on in your mind at the moment, whether positive or negative, constructive or critical. The best news of all is that if you change your thinking, you change your life. In fact, all great changes in your life begin with your changing your thinking in some specific way, for better or worse.

Think Like a Winner

Over the years, thousands of successful people have been asked, "What do you think about most of the time?"

Their answers tend to be the same worldwide. Successful people think about what they want and how to get it most of the time. As a result of this mental focus, they accomplish much more than the average person, even though they may have started with no particular advantages.

Unsuccessful people, on the other hand, tend to think and talk about what they don't want most of the time. They think and talk about who they are mad at and who is to blame for their problems most of the time. They don't understand why their lives don't improve even though they have been working as long as others. They slip into the habit of thinking and talking even more about their problems and who is to blame, thereby making the situation worse.

Martin Seligman of the University of Pennsylvania organized interviews with more than 350,000 men and women over a twenty-year period to find out how they thought most of the time. He summarized his findings in his best-selling book *Learned Optimism.*

What Seligman found was that the predominant quality of successful people is optimism. Successful people are far more optimistic most of the time than average people. They have a positive mental attitude toward themselves and others.

Your level of optimism is the very best predictor of how happy, healthy, wealthy, and long-lived you will be. The more optimistic and positive you are, the more energy and enthusiasm you will have. Your immune system will be stronger and more resistant to disease and infection. You will seldom be sick. You will get along with less sleep, and you will have more mental and physical energy throughout the day.

The more optimistic you are, the more creative you will be as well. You will constantly come up with great ideas and recognize new possibilities to help you move even faster toward your goals, the goals you think about most of the time.

Your determination to become a more optimistic person in every part of your life will do more to ensure your success and happiness than any other single quality you can develop.

The Focal Point Process requires that you continually put an "X" on the thought or activity that can be the most helpful to you at any given moment. As a general rule, your job is to keep your thinking optimistic and positive most of the time. This can be difficult, at least initially, but like any habit, you can develop it with repetition. When you practice thinking and responding optimistically most of the time, this positive attitude soon becomes a conditioned response. You will eventually find yourself reacting and responding positively and optimistically all day long.

Mental fitness and physical fitness are similar in certain ways. If you want to become physically fit, you have to work out physically. You have to exercise the different areas of your body, using cross-training to ensure maximum fitness from head to toe.

If you went to a health club and told the trainer that you wanted to become physically fit, he or she would show you how to use a variety of different pieces of equipment in a specific order, which would enable you to achieve a high level of fitness and maintain it over time.

Your level of optimism can be equated with your level of mental fitness. This form of mental fitness can be developed by practicing specific mental exercises, over and over, until you automatically respond in a positive and constructive way to anything that happens to you.

The Seven-Part Mental Fitness Program

There are seven mental exercises, or ways of thinking, that you can learn and practice every day to become a more positive, confident, and optimistic person. The more you think in these ways, the better you will feel, the more you will accomplish, and the faster and more easily you will accomplish it.

Think About the Future

The first and most important attitude you can practice to get the most out of yourself is *future orientation*. Future orientation is another of the most common characteristics of successful people, especially men and women who rise to positions of leadership and great responsibility in work, society, and personal life.

In 3,300 studies of leadership, seeking the common qualities possessed by great leaders through the ages, researchers found that the one quality all the studies had in common was *vision*. Leaders have vision. Nonleaders do not. Leaders have a vision of a better future for themselves, their families, and their organizations. They can see an ideal future in advance. They then work to make it a reality in the present.

Future-oriented people think about the future most of the time. They think about where they are going rather than where they have been. They think about what is possible in the months and years ahead rather than about the past, which cannot be changed.

Unfortunately, probably fewer than 10 percent of people in our society are genuinely future oriented. The vast majority are primarily concerned either about the present and the immediate gratification of the day and the evening or about the past and what has happened to them.

How can you tell whether a person is future oriented? Simply ask him or her, "If your life was perfect five years from now, what would it look like?" You can ask yourself this question as well.

Future-oriented people have an immediate answer to this question. Future-oriented people give a lot of thought to the future and what it will look like when they get there. Future-oriented people are very clear about what they *want* their lives to look like five years from now. Future-oriented people can *tell you* what they want and what they are working toward. They can tell you where they are going and *why* they want to go there. They have clear mental images of what they desire for their work, income, families, lifestyle, health, and levels of achievement in the years ahead.

Present- and past-oriented people tend to be vague and fuzzy about the future. They seldom think about it in detail. They often become offended if you ask them to describe their goals for the future.

In this respect, clarity is terribly important. Successful people have tremendous clarity about who they are, what they want, and how they are going to get it. Unsuccessful people usually are unsure and confused about who they are, what they want, and where they are going.

One powerful exercise you can practice to supercharge your thinking and accelerate your results is called *idealization*. In idealization you continually imagine the perfect outcome or solution for any situation in your life. You project forward three to five years, or even further, and then create a mental picture of the kind of life and career that would be ideal for you in every respect.

While you are visualizing and idealizing your perfect future, you let your mind float freely. You imagine for the moment that you have no limitations whatsoever on what you can be, do, or have.

Imagine that you have all the knowledge and experience you need. Imagine that you have all the money and resources you need. Imagine that you have all the friends and contacts you want. Imagine that all opportunities and possibilities are open to you. Imagine that if you can dream it, you can do it.

Develop a dream list. Write down everything you would like to have in your life and work sometime in the future, as if your goals were guaranteed in some way if only you could be clear about them.

If you are married, sit down with your spouse to make up this dream list. Ask, "What would we do, how would we change our lives, if we won ten million dollars, tax free, tomorrow?"

If you had all the time and money you wanted and you could be or have anything at all in life, what would you really want? The greater clarity you can achieve in describing your ideal future, the more likely you are to create that future for yourself, and usually faster than you can imagine right now. However, you can't hit a target you can't see. Clarity is essential.

Create a Five-Year Vision

As business sage Peter Drucker wrote, "We greatly overestimate what we can do in one year. But we greatly underestimate what is possible for us in five years."

When I conduct strategic planning exercises for corporations, I always begin with this exercise. I ask the executives to imagine that their company is perfect five years from today. I ask them to imagine that a special news story is going to be written on this company and published in the national press. I ask them, "How would this company be described if it was the very best company of its kind in the entire industry?"

We then go around the room and write down the answers to this question on flipcharts or whiteboards. We often generate twenty or thirty ideal descriptions of the company five years from now. We then discuss and prioritize the answers. We determine which are more important and which are less important. We determine which are inputs and which are outputs, which are causes and which are effects. Finally, we agree on the three to five most important ideal visions that this company could fulfill in five years. With this vision statement clarified, we then begin to set strategy by asking, "How?"

"How" is one of the most important and powerful words you can learn and apply to every situation in your life. Once you have a clear vision of what you want, the only question you ask is, "How do I achieve it?"

Asking *how* forces you to be both positive and future oriented. The word "how" triggers creativity in youself and others. The regular use of the word "how" is like stepping on the accelerator of your mind and revving up the engine of your personal genius. The more you ask "How?" to any question, goal, or dream, the more insights and ideas you will have to turn your visions into realities.

The best news of all is that when you think about the future and think about how you can make your future ideal a current reality, you become more optimistic and positive about the present. You experience greater energy and enthusiasm. You feel a heightened sense of confidence and personal power. You become more motivated and committed. You communicate with greater clarity and effectiveness.

A group of people united around a common vision, with a total commitment to making it come true, can form the nucleus of a powerful team or company. This future vision motivates and inspires people to perform at higher levels than ever before. This ideal image or picture serves as a guide and a directional mechanism for both individual and corporate decision making.

Take a Test Every Day

All of life is a test in some way. You are constantly being tested by the ups and downs and unexpected events of daily life. The way you respond to the world around you is the way in which you take and pass this test.

Perhaps the greatest test of all is your ability to think and talk about the future, about what you want and where you are going, most of the time. This must become the focal point in your thinking. This is the "X" that determines the direction of your life. This is the test you pass or fail depending on what you choose to think about most of the time.

Think About Your Goals

The second attitude of highly successful people is *goal orientation*. Successful people think about their goals and how they can achieve them most of the time. Unsuccessful people think about their problems and spend their time criticizing, complaining, and making excuses most of the time.

Future orientation deals with your long-term ideal vision. Goal orientation is more precise. You take your visions out of the air and translate them into specific and tangible actions and measures that you can implement immediately. Henry David Thoreau put it aptly, "Have you built your castles in the air? Good, that is where they should be built. Now go to work and build foundations under them."

Three percent: That is about how many adults actually put their goals into writing. The other 97 percent have wishes, hopes, and fantasies. People without goals are doomed to work forever for people who do have goals.

The key to goal setting is for you to think on paper. Successful men and women think with a pen in their hands; unsuccessful people do not. When you write things down, you crystallize them right before your eyes. They become tangible and concrete. They become subject to positive manipulation and definite action. Written goals activate your positive mind and energize you. Written goals release powers within you that would have lain dormant in their absence. The act of writing them down increases enormously the likelihood that you will achieve your goals.

Setting goals is straightforward. It is a definite skill you can learn through practice. Once you have mastered the process and practice of goal setting, you will be able to step on the accelerator of your own life and make more progress in the next year or two than you may have made in the last ten years.

Seven Steps to Goal Setting

Here is a simple seven-step formula for setting and achieving goals that you can use for the rest of your career:

1. Decide exactly what you want in each area of your life. Most people never do this. Clarity is essential.

2. Write it down clearly and specifically. Make it measurable. Here's an example: *To increase my income by 50 percent in the next two years.* A goal that is not in writing is merely a fantasy. It has no energy behind it.

3. Set a deadline for your goal and, if necessary, set subdeadlines. Your subconscious mind thrives on time-specific goals. For example: I will achieve half my income goal within eleven months and the other half within two years.

4. Make a list of everything you will have to do to achieve your goal. Add to your list as you think of new activities and tasks, which you will. Keep adding to your list until it is complete.

5. Organize your list into a plan. Decide what you need to do first and what you need to do later. Decide what must be done and in what order. Rework your plan until it is complete.

6. Take action on your plan immediately. Do something, do anything, but get started. It is amazing how many people fail because they don't take action on their goals and plans.

7. Resolve to do something every day that moves you toward your major goal, whatever it is at the moment. This discipline of doing something every day enables you to develop and maintain momentum. Daily action increases your determination and gives you energy. This single resolution, daily action, can turn your life around.

Once you have determined your goals and written them down, think about them all the time, morning, noon, and night. And the only question you ask is, "How?" How can you achieve them? "Whether" is no longer a question for you.

Commit to Excellence

The third attitude for great success is *excellence orientation*. By definition, successful people are very good at what they do. You must also become very good at your job. Commit to excellence in your work. Resolve today to join the top 10 percent in your field, no matter how much effort and sacrifice is necessary and no matter how long it takes.

For many years, because of my limited background and my low self-esteem, it never occurred to me that I could be good at anything. Even if I did well occasionally, I would dismiss it as being a matter of luck or coincidence. I often felt like an impostor when people congratulated me for doing something well. Then, when I was twenty-eight, I had a revelation that changed my life. It may change yours as well.

I learned that everyone in the top 10 percent of his or her field had to start somewhere, most of them in the bottom 10 percent. I found out that everyone who is doing well today, in any area, was once doing poorly by comparison. I also realized that everyone who is leading in his or her profession or occupation today was at one time not even in that profession or occupation.

Life is very much like a buffet line. Life is self-serve. Nobody brings it to you. You cannot sit at the table and bang your knife and fork for service. You have to get up, accept responsibility, and serve yourself.

If you want to get to the front of the buffet line of life, two steps are necessary. First, get in line! Make a decision to be excellent at what you do and then get in line. From that moment on, do something every day to improve.

Second, stay in line. Don't make an occasional attempt at personal improvement and then go back and watch television. Get in line and stay in line. Keep putting one foot in front of the other. Learn and practice new things every single day. Keep moving forward. Never lose your momentum.

The good news is that the buffet line of life never closes. It is open twenty-four hours a day. Anyone can get in line and stay in line. Anyone can decide to become the best in his or her field and then begin working toward that goal.

It doesn't matter how long it takes. If you stay in line, if you continue getting a little better each day, nothing and no one but you yourself can stop you from eventually getting to the front of the line. No one but you can stop you from joining the top 10 percent in your field. It's completely up to you. You can be either your best friend or your worst enemy by the decisions you make or fail to make.

When you become excellent at what you do, your life will change completely. Your self-esteem, self-respect, and personal pride will increase dramatically. You will feel terrific about yourself. You will be respected and admired by all the people around you.

Here's the key focal point question: *"What one skill, if you developed and did it in an excellent fashion, would help you the most in your career?"*

This is where you put the "X" in your personal and professional development. This is what you think and talk about most of the time. This is what you dedicate yourself to accomplishing all day long.

Nothing will help you to fulfill your vision and achieve your goals faster than becoming excellent at the most important thing you could possibly do in your work. And you almost always know what that is.

Whatever your most important desired skill is, set it as a goal, write it down, make a plan, and work on it every day. A week, a month, a year from now, you will look around you and be absolutely amazed at the progress you have made in your life and your career.

Focus on Results

The fourth attitude you need to develop for optimism and outstanding personal performance is *result orientation*. Successful people think constantly about the results that are expected of them. They are constantly writing and planning and setting priorities on their most important tasks.

Result orientation is a critical part of the Focal Point Process. In result orientation, you make a list of everything you have to do before you begin. You organize your list by priority and value. You select the most important thing you could possibly do and then you concentrate single-mindedly on accomplishing that one task. You persevere without diversion or distraction until it is complete.

Intense result orientation goes hand in hand with high productivity, high performance, and high output. Result orientation is based on your asking and answering the following four questions, over and over, every minute and hour of every day:

1. *What are my highest-value activities?* What are the things you do that contribute the greatest value to your work? If you are not sure, make a list of all of your tasks and responsibilities and take them to your boss. Discuss them with your colleagues and coworkers. You must be absolutely clear about the most important results that are expected of you. Remember, *the very worst use of time is to do very well what needs not be done at all.*

2. *What are my key result areas?* What are the results that you absolutely, positively, have to get in an excellent fashion to fulfill your responsibilities and do your job well? There are seldom more than five to seven key result areas in any job. Your first responsibility is to identify these key results, to set standards of performance for each result area. You then dedicate yourself to working every day to meet those standards. What gets measured gets done. If you can't measure it, you can't manage it.

3. *What can I and only I do that, if done well, will make a real difference to my company?* There is only one answer to this question at any given time. This is a job that you and only you can do. If you don't do it, it won't get done. No one else can do it for you. But if you do it, and do it well, it can make a significant contribution to your company and your career. What is it?

4. *What is the most valuable use of my time?* This is the most important question in time management. You should ask and answer this question every hour of every day. What is the most valuable use of your time right now? Asking and answering this question is the key to peak performance. Whatever your answer to this question, be sure that you are working on this particular task every minute of every hour. Compared with this task, everything else is a relative waste of time.

In the final analysis, getting results is everything. The quality and quantity of your results determine the quality and quantity of your rewards. The Focal Point Process requires that you continually put an "X" on the one task or activity that is more valuable and important than any other. You then discipline yourself to work single-mindedly on that one task until it is complete.

Concentrate on Solutions

The fifth attitude for optimism and high performance is *solution orientation,* in which you think about the solution to the problem most of the time. You think about what can be done and how the problem can be solved instead of what has happened and who is to blame.

Unsucessful people think and talk about their problems most of the time. The more you think and talk about your problems, the more negative, angry, and pessimistic you become. But when you think and talk about the *solutions,* you become positive, creative, and optimistic.

Life is a continuous succession of problems. They never end. They come in like the waves of the ocean, one after another. In addition, if you are living a normal, busy life today, you will probably have a *crisis* of some kind every two or three months. The only thing that really matters is how effectively you respond when things go wrong.

Your ability to solve problems largely determines your success and your income. This ability determines how far you go and how high you rise in life. No matter what the title on your business card, you can cross it off and write "Problem Solver." That's what you are. That's what you do, all day long. The only question is, "How good are you at problem solving?"

Highly successful people solve big problems. Unsuccessful people solve little problems or no problems at all. And the bigger and more expensive the problems you solve, the larger and more important are the problems you will be given to solve.

The key to becoming an excellent problem solver is to think and talk about possible solutions most of the time. Whenever something goes wrong, resist the temptation to become angry, blame others, or make excuses. Instead, ask questions like, "What's the solution? What do we do now? What is the next step? How do we solve this problem? How do we limit the damage? How can we prevent this from happening again? Where do we go from here?"

The good news is that the more you focus on solutions, the better you become at discovering even better and more complex solutions. You become more effective and creative in everything you do by focusing on solutions most of the time. Your mind functions at a higher level.

This is one of the great breakthrough discoveries in brain physiology. A truly effective person is one who has developed a wonderful ability to respond constructively to the inevitable problems and difficulties of day-to-day life. This must be your goal as well. Think about solutions all day long.

Dedicate Yourself to Lifelong Learning

The sixth attitude of optimistic people is *growth orientation.* This fact is: *Your life gets better only when you get better*.

Growth-oriented people are committed to themselves and to their futures. They are eager to learn and practice new ideas, insights, techniques, methods, and strategies. They are hungry for new information. Like sponges, they soak up everything they can from every source around them.

Basketball coach Pat Riley wrote, "If you're not getting better, you're getting worse."

You have enormous untapped reserves of mental capacity that you have never used. You have the ability to learn and become excellent in more areas than you can ever dream of. But your mind is like a muscle. If you don't use it, you lose it, at least temporarily.

The future belongs to the competent. In the twenty-first century, the future belongs to the omnicompetent. The future belongs to people who are very good at what they do and who are getting better every single day.

To earn more, you must learn more. You must add more value. You must develop the ability to make a better and more important contribution. You must be asking, every single day, "What can I do to increase my value to my company today?"

Here's a powerful practice that can move you to the top of your field and make you a great success in whatever you undertake. *Invest 3 percent of your income back into yourself for the rest of your life.* This 3 percent formula is miraculous! For every dollar you invest in your mind, in becoming better at what you do, you can eventually earn $10, $20, $30, $50, sometimes even $100 back in personal income.

Many of my students have told me about investing in a single book or audio program that has paid for itself 1,000 times, 2,000 times, and even 5,000 times over in as little as a year. A thirty-five-year-old father of two with an eighth-grade education, working out of his home, purchased a $60 audio program to help his business. In the next ten months, he increased his income from $30,000 to $304,000. Personal development can really pay off!

You are your most valuable asset. Your ability to think well and act effectively depends on the quality and quantity of knowledge and ideas available to you. You must continually feed your mind to develop more of your potential. You must continually upgrade your abilities to think and perform at higher levels.

Here is a simple formula for lifelong success that can make you rich: Invest as much in your mind each year as you invest in your car.

If you spend as much money upgrading your skills and abilities each year as you spend to keep your car on the road, you could become one of the most competent and highest-paid people in America, if not the world.

The three keys to growth orientation are simple. First, read one hour or more each day in your chosen field. The highest-paid people in America read two to three hours each day to keep current and improve their minds. But if you read only one hour per day from a good book that helps you to be better at your job, that would be enough.

Second, listen to audio programs in your car, when you exercise, and when you move around. The average car owner sits in his or her car 500 to 1,000 hours each year. If you listen to educational audio programs as you drive from place to place, you can get the equivalent of full-time university attendance. This practice alone can make you one of the best-informed and highest-paid people in your field.

Third, attend every helpful course and seminar you can find, even if you have to pay a lot or travel great distances. Countless highly paid professionals in every field have told me that the turning point in their lives came when they sacrificed to attend a seminar where they learned something that changed their thinking forever.

Retire Ten Years Early
Some years ago, my dentist made a great sacrifice of time and money to attend an international dentistry conference in Hong Kong. In one of the concurrent sessions, he learned a

technique in cosmetic dentistry that had just been developed. He immediately began using it on his patients, including me. He soon became known as the expert in this specialized area. Patients, including other dentists, came to him from great distances.

Five years later he sold his practice and retired as a multi-millionaire, at age fifty-one. He has never worked since. He lives in a beautiful home overlooking the ocean and enjoys a wonderful life. He told me that that one scientific break-through transformed his practice and made him one of the highest-paid and most successful dentists of his generation.

If you believe in yourself and your future, you will invest in yourself and your abilities. The converse is also true. The more you invest in yourself, the more you will believe in yourself. Each reinforces the other.

Think every day about the most important subject you could learn to help yourself to achieve your most important goal. Put an "X" on this particular area of knowledge or skill. Think about it and study it every day. Work on developing yourself in that area continually. Work on yourself as though your entire future depended on it, because it does.

Do It Now!

The seventh attitude of the highest-paid people in every field is *action orientation*. Resolve today to develop a sense of urgency in your work. It would be overstatement to say that more than 2 percent of working adults have a sense of urgency, and it is this tiny minority that eventually rises to the top of every field of endeavor.

Everyone today is in a hurry. Everyone is impatient. For this reason, people often equate speed with quality. If you act fast when they have a need or a question, they automatically assume that your work is better and of higher value than that of someone who moves slowly. By moving fast, you gain a competitive edge.

Resolve to move quickly when opportunity or necessity presents itself. Develop and maintain a fast tempo in your work. Keep stepping on the accelerator of your own potential. Become a moving target.

The faster you move, the more energy you have. The faster you move, the more experience you get. The more experience you get, the faster you learn. The faster you learn, the better you get. And the better you get, the more you will be paid and the faster you will be promoted.

The faster you move, the greater is your self-esteem, self-respect, and personal pride. The faster you move, the more valued and respected you will be among the people around you. The faster you move, the better will be the quality of your life in almost every area.

....

To recap this chapter, remember that you become what you think about most of the time. Successful, happy, highly paid people think and talk about what they want and how to get it most of the time.

Successful people *think about the future*. They idealize, visualize, and imagine what their ideal futures will look like. Then they work to make their visions into their realities.

Highly productive people are intensely *goal oriented*. They decide what they want, write it down, set a deadline, make a plan, and then work on it every day.

The highest paid people are *excellence oriented.* They are very good at what they do, and they are constantly getting better. They are dedicated to working in the one skill area that can help them make the greatest contribution in their work.

The most successful people are *result oriented.* They are intensely focused on getting the most important results expected from them in their work. They are continually increasing their value by doing more and more things of greater and greater importance.

Optimistic people are intensely *solution oriented* as well. They think about solutions rather than problems. They keep their minds positive, creative, and forward thinking by always looking for ways to solve problems rather than blaming someone else for them. And the bigger the problems they solve, the bigger problems they are given to solve.

The multiplier that makes all the other orientations work is *growth orientation.* You are your most precious resource. You are your most valuable asset. The more you invest in yourself, the greater will be your return in both money and satisfaction. Develop yourself continually, day after day, exactly as if you were in an intense competition, and in danger of losing, because you are.

Finally, become *action oriented* in your work and personal life. Overcome procrastination and get started immediately on your key tasks. Keep repeating to yourself, "Do it now! Do it now!"

By taking complete control of your mind and keeping your thinking focused on exactly the things you want and how to get them, you will move ahead faster and with greater certainty than by doing anything else.

CHAPTER FIVE

Practice Personal Strategic Planning

Nothing can add more power to your life than concentrating all your energies on a limited set of targets.

—NIDO QUBEIN

A s discussed in earlier chapters, your ability to think, plan, decide, and take action determines the entire course of your life. The better you become in each area, the better will be each part of your life and the faster you will achieve your goals.

Personal strategic planning is the tool you use to get from wherever you are to wherever you want to go. The difference between using personal strategic planning as a central part of your life and just letting your life happen without a plan is like the difference between driving a car and riding a bicycle. Both will get you from point A to point B, but the car, personal strategic planning, will get you there much faster and easier.

Fortunately, personal strategic planning is a systematic way of thinking and acting. It is therefore learnable, like learning to type or drive a car. There are many different elements of this key skill, but with practice you can get into the rhythm of thinking and acting strategically for the rest of your life. When you do, your life and career will take off like a rocket.

The Benefits of a Good Strategy

Some years ago, I was invited to take the executive group of a young, dynamic New York Stock Exchange company through a two-day strategic planning exercise. This company had grown rapidly, largely through the ambition and drive of the top managers. The company was experiencing a booming market, and the managers were intensely motivated by the potential for high personal incomes.

None of them, including the president of the company, had ever done any strategic planning before. At that time, their annual sales were about $75 million. Their goal for the next year, a stretch goal, was to increase sales to $100 million.

Most of the key people were in their late twenties. They were skeptical of the whole idea of strategic planning. They thought it was largely a waste of time. After all, they reasoned, they knew what they needed to get done and they thought they were doing a pretty good job.

For two days, I helped them to ask and answer a series of questions about themselves, their business, their market, and their future. As they wrestled with these questions and argued with each other, they quickly realized that they had been succeeding largely on the basis of luck, energy, and a good market. As a result, they got seriously into the work of strategic planning and hammered out a clear set of goals and plans for the coming year.

The result was amazing. Instead of increasing their sales from $75 million to $100 million, which most of them had considered optimistic, they hit $125 million in revenues within the next twelve months. They told me later that they attributed their entire success to the two days we spent together in strategic planning.

Strategic Planning Saves Time and Money

The reason that strategic planning is so helpful is that it saves you an enormous amount of time and money. By thinking through the key questions and concepts of strategy, you very quickly find yourself doing more and more of the most important tasks that can move you toward your key goals. At the same time, you do fewer and fewer of the things that are not particularly helpful. You do more things right and fewer things wrong. You establish specific targets for the company and for everyone in it. You greatly improve your ability to measure and track results. You move onto the fast track in your work and in your life in general.

The purpose of corporate strategic planning is to increase return on equity. *Equity* is defined as the amount of shareholder money invested and working in the enterprise. The aim of strategic planning in business is to reorganize and restructure the activities of the corporation to achieve a higher quality and quantity of outputs relative to inputs, to improve profitability.

Overall, the goal of strategic planning is to enable the company to use its people and resources more effectively. The company will then function better than before. It will outperform its competition. This improvement can be measured in terms of higher sales, greater market share, better profitability, higher returns on invested assets, and better positioning for the future.

Designing Your Life and Career

Personal strategic planning is very similar to corporate strategic planning. However, instead of return on equity, personal strategic planning is aimed at increasing your *return on energy*. Put another way, it increases your return on *life*.

The equity in a business is measured in terms of financial capital. Your personal equity, on the other hand, is measured in terms of your own human capital.

Your personal equity is composed of the mental, emotional, and physical energies you have to invest in your career. Your goal should be to get the highest return possible on the investment of yourself in everything you do. How well you invest yourself determines your income. This is the focal point of personal strategic planning.

You can tell that it is time to revisit your strategic plan when you are no longer getting the results you want from your work or from your life. When you feel frustrated or dissatisfied, this is often an indication that you should sit down and ask yourself some good, hard questions. When you experience resistance or stress or find yourself working harder and harder only to feel that you are getting fewer and fewer rewards, you should stand back and consider revising your strategy.

The Sigmoid Curve

Life moves in regular cycles, like the seasons. Most human activities follow what is called the sigmoid curve. This curve is like the letter *S,* lying on its side. Every new endeavor begins at the high point of the *S* on the left, declines as it goes through a learning phase, rises as it goes through a growth phase, levels off at the top, and then declines again (see Figure 5-1).

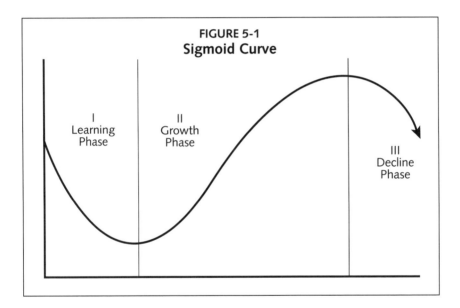

FIGURE 5-1
Sigmoid Curve

I
Learning
Phase

II
Growth
Phase

III
Decline
Phase

The sigmoid curve applies to product and service cycles, personal and professional relationships, careers, corporation life cycles, and even the histories of nations and empires.

It is helpful for you to stand back and identify where each part of your life is today on the sigmoid curve. Are you in phase I, the learning phase? Are you in phase II, the growth phase? Or are you in phase III, the decline phase?

In phase I, you are extraordinarily busy, facing challenges and difficulties, learning and trying new things as you scramble to get results, especially financial results. In phase II, the growth phase, you are in a state of high energy and exhilaration, with business and sales growing and all kinds of new possibilities and ideas bubbling up on all sides. In phase III, the excitement starts to go out of the business or your career. You are selling fewer products or services or achieving fewer results or rewards. Profit margins are smaller and harder to earn. There is a vague sense of "Is this all there is?"

Seven Questions in Strategic Planning

There are seven key questions in strategic planning, both for you and for your business. These are questions that you need to ask and answer over and over, throughout your career. Sometimes a new answer to any of these questions can dramatically change the direction of your business and your life. Insights that you get from continually asking these questions can lead you to establish new goals and new focal points for your future.

Define Your Business or Career Clearly

The first and most important question is, *"What business am I in?"* What business are you *really* in? Define your business in terms of what you *do* for your customer or your company. Keep expanding the definition of your business so that it is as broad as possible. Never be satisfied with the first answer.

For example, railroads defined themselves as being in the business of moving people and freight by rail. In reality, they were in the transportation business. By ignoring the other avenues of transportation that were developing, such as trucks, buses, ships, and airplanes, many railroads went out of business.

Many Internet companies defined themselves as providers of free information geared toward attracting as many eyeballs as possible. In reality, the Internet is a communication and distribution channel that must be focused on selling products or services and making a profit, like any other business. This failure to accurately define the business has led to the loss of many billions of investment dollars and market capitalization.

Define your business in terms of the effect your products or services have on the life or work of other people or organizations. By the same token, define your personal work in terms of the effect you have on the people you work for and with.

Once you have decided clearly what business you are in, apply zero-based thinking to your activities and ask, "Knowing what I now know, is there anything I am doing today that I wouldn't get into again if I had to do it over?"

As Peter Drucker says, "Planning for tomorrow means sloughing off yesterday. Before you can do something new, you have to stop doing something old."

Creating the future means leaving the past behind. Keep asking yourself, "What are the activities that I should reduce, discontinue, or avoid altogether, based on the situation the way it really is today?"

Think About the Future

The next question to ask is, *"What business will I be in if things continue the way they are today?"*

If you do not change, what will you be doing one year, two years, and five years from today? Is it an intelligent strategy to continue in your current line of business, or should you be looking at changing in some way?

What business *should* you be in? Look at yourself, your talents, your abilities, your ambitions, your energies, and especially your heart's desire to determine the business you should be in, the work you should be doing sometime in the future.

What business *could* you be in? If you were to dramatically change your level of knowledge or skills, your products or services, your industries or markets, what business could you be in if you really wanted to be? What changes would you have to make today to create the business of the future? What changes will you have to make personally to become the kind of person who can live the life and do the work you would really like to be doing sometime in the future?

Identify Your Customers

The third question is, *"Who is my customer?"* Whom do you have to satisfy in order to survive and thrive in your career? Of course, your first customer is your boss, the person who signs your paycheck. Your primary job at work is to make sure that you are satisfying his or her essential needs. Do you know what they are?

You can define a customer as anyone who depends on you for his or her success and anyone you depend on for your success. Under this definition, your colleagues and your staff are also your customers. Everyone around you whom you help, or who helps you, is a customer in some way.

Who is your external customer, the customer who uses what you produce? This is the focal point of business success. Your ability to accurately identify the external customer whose satisfaction determines your success in your career is critical to every element of strategic planning.

What does your customer value? What specific benefits does your customer get from using your products or services? What does your customer want and need from you to be completely satisfied? How does your product change or improve his or her life and work?

The twenty-first century has been called the Age of the Customer. The customer is king or queen. Your ability to identify and satisfy your key customers is a critical determinant of your success and your rewards in life.

Who will your customer be in the future if current trends continue? Who *should* your customer be if you want to rise to the top of your field? Who *could* your customer be if you were to change your product or service offerings? How could you upgrade your knowledge and skills and your ability to satisfy that customer?

Fire Your Customers

Are there any customers in your business, whom, knowing what you now know, you wouldn't start working with again today? Answering this question honestly is an essential part of liberating yourself and your company from some of the decisions of the past.

Many companies today are analyzing and identifying the qualities and characteristics of their very best customers. They are then sorting their customers into high-value and low-value customer segments. By doing this, they can focus more of their time and attention on their highest-value customers and on acquiring more customers like them. Simultaneously, they spend less time on their lower-value customers, and in many cases they encourage their lower-value customers to do business with other companies.

Not long ago, a friend of mine, a successful entrepreneur, applied the 80/20 Rule to his customer base. He determined that 20 percent of his customers contributed 80 percent of his sales volume and 80 percent of his profits. He decided to "fire" the 80 percent of his customers who contributed 20 percent or less of his revenues. One by one, he handed them off to other companies in his industry whom he felt could serve them better. He then focused all his attention on his higher-value customers. Within a year, his business and his personal income doubled. Would this strategy work for you?

Identify Your Area of Excellence

The fourth question is this: *"What do I do especially well?"* What is your area of excellence, your area of superiority? What is your personal competitive advantage over the other people in your field?

This is a vital question in personal strategic planning. You will be truly successful only to the degree that you become excellent at the most important part of your work. One of your chief responsibilities in life is to select the area of excellence that can have the greatest positive impact on your career and your income, and then throw your whole heart into becoming very, very good in that one area.

In *Competing for the Future,* Gary Hamel points out that the top companies are those that project forward five years and then identify the core competencies they will need at that time to dominate their industries. They then implement a development plan to ensure that they have those core competencies in place when the future arrives.

You should follow this strategy as well. What are the core competencies you will need to be in the top 10 percent of your field three to five years from now? How do they differ from your key skills today? What can you do today to begin developing those additional skills and abilities? Whatever competencies you will need to be the best, set them as a goal, make a plan, and begin working on developing them every day.

Focus on Your Highest-Value Activities

The fifth question in personal strategic planning is this: *"What are the 10 to 20 percent of my activities that could account for 80 to 90 percent of my results?"* What are the tasks you do today that yield the highest returns and rewards relative to the cost and effort of performing those activities? How can you organize your work life so that you are doing more and more of these higher-value tasks (see Figure 5-2)?

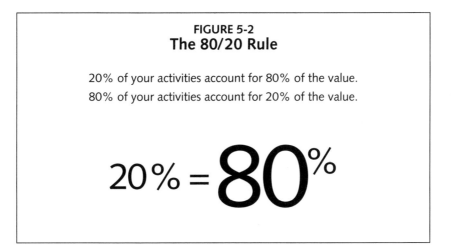

FIGURE 5-2
The 80/20 Rule

20% of your activities account for 80% of the value.
80% of your activities account for 20% of the value.

$$20\% = 80\%$$

Remove Your Key Constraints

The sixth question in personal strategic planning is this: *"What are the critical constraints on my ability to achieve my goals?"*

In every work or production process, there are a series of steps between where you are today and the result you want to achieve tomorrow. Invariably, one of these steps is the constraint or chokepoint that determines the speed at which you complete the process and achieve your goal (see Figure 5-3).

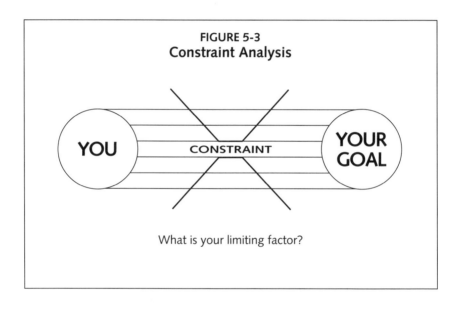

FIGURE 5-3
Constraint Analysis

YOU — CONSTRAINT — YOUR GOAL

What is your limiting factor?

For example, between your home and your office, there may be a stretch of road or freeway that sometimes is extremely crowded. Before that stretch and after that stretch, the traffic is light. But if that stretch is jammed, this can be the major bottleneck that determines how fast you cover the entire distance.

If your goal is to double your income, the first thing to do is identify the different steps you must take to get from the income you have today to the income you want. You then examine each of these steps and determine which step is the limiting factor that determines how fast you achieve your income goal.

Ask yourself, "Why aren't I at my goal already?"

If you want to double your income, why aren't you earning twice as much already? If you want to spend more time with your family or friends, why aren't you doing it already? Often, forcing yourself to develop the answers to these questions will enable you to see the critical constraint that is holding you back.

Here is an important point. I would contend that fully 80 percent of all the constraints that are holding you back from achieving your most desired goals are inside you. Only 20 percent are on the outside. Fully 80 percent of the reasons that your company is not achieving its goals are inside the company, in some way. Fully 80 percent of the reasons that you are not making more money or increasing your free time are within yourself. Your major constraints usually lie within your own habits, beliefs, attitudes, opinions, skills, and abilities.

When you want to accomplish great things, you always start with yourself and work out from there. Ask yourself, "What is it *in me* that is holding me back?" You are in control of yourself. You can have an enormous effect on what you do personally or fail to do. But you have only a minor influence on external factors and other people. Always start with yourself.

Choose to Take Action

The seventh question in personal strategic planning is, *"What specific action or actions am I going to take immediately based on my answers to these questions?"* The purpose of strategic thinking and planning is to choose the actions you are going to take to bring about different results from what you are achieving today. What are they?

Sharpen Your Focus

Here are several additional questions that you should ask and answer regularly as part of your personal strategic planning:

■ If you could wave a magic wand and have whatever you wished for in any part of your life, what would it be?

■ If you could design your perfect lifestyle, day in and day out, what would it look like?

■ If you could create your perfect calendar, how would you spend each day, each week, each month, and each year?

■ How would you change your life if you received $1 million cash, tax free, today? What is the first thing you would do?

■ What parts of your work do you enjoy the most and do the best? Where do you excel? What sorts of activities make you the happiest?

■ What would you do, how would you spend your time, if you learned today that you had only six months left to live?

■ What one great thing would you dare to dream if you knew you could not fail? If you were absolutely guaranteed success in any one goal, small or large, short term or long term, what would it be?

When you ask and answer these questions honestly, you dramatically increase your awareness of who you are and what you want. Invariably, you will find that there are things you are doing today that you should stop doing as soon as possible. In addition, you will realize that there are things you should be doing more of and new activities that you should be starting.

The personal strategic planning process for Focal Point divides your life into seven areas. This enables you to clarify what you want in each area and what you have to do to get the things you want. The seven areas of life are the following:

1. *Business and career:* How do you become extremely successful and satisfied and move to the top of your field?

2. *Family and personal life:* How do you achieve balance between external success and your personal relationships?

3. *Money and investments:* How do you get your financial life under control and achieve financial independence?

4. *Health and fitness:* How do you achieve and maintain high levels of fitness, energy, and overall well-being?

5. *Personal growth and development:* How do you identify and acquire the key knowledge and skills that you need to live an extraordinary life?

6. *Social and community activities:* How do you structure your life so that you make a real difference in the world and leave a lasting legacy?

7. *Spiritual development and inner peace:* How do you organize your inner life and thinking so that you realize your full potential as a human being?

Give yourself a grade in each area, on a scale of 1 to 10, with 1 being the lowest and 10 being the highest. You will find that most of your stress and unhappiness comes in the area where you give yourself the lowest grade. Once you identify that area, you can determine the specific steps you need to take to get that area under control.

The Focal Point Process

The Focal Point Process consists of seven steps in each area. These seven steps make up a system of personal strategic planning that enables you to determine where to the put the "X" in each part of your life. They are the following:

1. *Values:* What are the values, virtues, qualities, and traits that are most important to you in each area of your life?

2. *Vision:* If your life were perfect in this area five years from today, what would it look like?

3. *Goals:* What specific goals must you achieve to fulfill your ideal future vision in that area?

4. *Knowledge and skills:* In what areas will you have to excel in the future to achieve your goals and fulfill your vision?

5. *Habits:* What specific habits of thought and action do you need to become the person who is capable of achieving the goals you have set for yourself?

6. *Daily activities:* What specific activities do you have to engage in each day to ensure that you become the person you want to become and achieve the goals you want to achieve?

7. *Actions:* What specific action or actions are you going to take immediately to begin realizing your ideal future vision?

In the rest of this book, we will deal with each of these questions and each of the seven areas in detail. Step by step, you will develop absolute clarity about what you want in every part of your life. You will learn how to set clear priorities in each category. You will identify specific actions you can take immediately to bring about powerful and positive change in your life.

The quality of your thinking determines the quality of your life. The better questions you ask yourself, the better answers you will elicit. As you improve the quality of your thinking, the quality of everything you do improves at the same time. Because there is no limit to how much you can improve the quality of your thinking, there is no real limit to how much you can improve your life.

The law of correspondence says that your outer world will always reflect your inner world. To change anything in your outer world, you must begin by changing what is going on in your inner world.

The greater clarity you have with regard to who you are, what you want, and what you have to do to get it, the faster you will move ahead. You will accomplish much more, and your life will be better in every area.

CHAPTER SIX

Supercharge Your Business and Career

You can do anything you wish to do, have anything you wish to have, be anything you wish to be.

—ROBERT COLLIER

Once upon a time, people grew up, got a job, and worked at it for the rest of their lives with little variation. But those days are gone forever.

According to the experts, a person starting work today will have, on average, fourteen full-time jobs lasting two years or more and five careers in completely different fields or industries. According to a study cited in *Fortune* magazine not too long ago, 42 percent of the workforce is made up of "free agents."

These are contingency workers who will move from company to company throughout their careers.

Each year, more than 1 million new businesses start up in the United States. These are in addition to the more than 20 million businesses that already exist. On top of that, hundreds of thousands of new partnerships, joint ventures, and sole proprietorships are formed each year. Tens of thousands of new products, processes, and services are introduced into an already crowded marketplace. Millions of people move up, down, or sideways in their jobs, companies, or careers. The rate of change, growth, and expanding opportunity has never been greater and, if anything, it is getting better every year.

Here are three predictions for you: First, there will be more changes in your field, whatever it is, in the year ahead than ever before. Second, there will be more competition in your field than ever before. And third, there will be more opportunities in your field than ever before, but they will be different from those of today and in different areas than you expect or anticipate.

As many as 72 percent of people working today will be in a different job within the next two years as a result of the incredible speed of change, increase in competition, and explosion of opportunity. As many as 50 percent of working people today are in the first year of their current jobs. Whatever you are doing, your job responsibilities and outputs probably have changed dramatically in the last few months, and they will continue to change.

Andrew Grove, chairman of Intel Corporation, wrote recently that one of the most profound changes of the last decade is that each person today is now the architect of his or her own career. You can no longer rely on a corporation to take care of you and accept responsibility for your long-term success in your work life. You must think and act for yourself.

As mentioned in Chapter One, you are the president of your own personal services corporation. You are always self-employed, no matter who signs your paycheck. The biggest mistake you can ever make is to ever think that you work for anyone but yourself. The key to your success in whatever you do is to see yourself as an independent agent. You must continually look for ways to add value, every single day. You are responsible.

A sense of control is the key to a positive mental attitude and a feeling of personal power. When you accept complete responsibility for your life, you take control of your destiny and you feel terrific about yourself. You feel stronger, more confident, and more powerful. You become a master of circumstances rather than merely a victim of circumstances.

Your primary responsibility to yourself is to design your future the way you want it to be. Clarity is essential. The very act of becoming clear about what you want and what you have to do to get it dramatically increases the likelihood that you will realize your goals exactly as you imagined and on schedule.

The Focal Point Process helps you to identify exactly what is most important to you. It helps you identify what you need to do to achieve your most important goals. It enables you to determine the steps you have to take to get from wherever you are to wherever you want to go.

Determine Your Business and Career Values

The starting point of business success for both individuals and organizations lies in *value clarification*. Value clarification is an exercise that enables you to determine what principles are important to you and in what order. You then build your career on the foundation of these values.

People are happiest and most fulfilled when their lives are consistent with their highest values and their innermost convictions. High-performing people are clear about what they believe and stand for, and they don't deviate from these values.

Unhappy, underachieving people are often fuzzy or confused about their values, and they compromise them regularly.

You live from the inside out. The core of your being is composed of your deepest beliefs about what is right and good in the human condition. Your values determine your emotions, your motivations, and your responses to the world around you. Your values determine the kind of people you like, love, are attracted to, and enjoy working and living with. Your values determine the activities you most enjoy and what sort of work you will excel at.

You identify most strongly with people whose values are consistent with your own. You fall in love with a person who has the same values you do. You enjoy working for a company and with people who share your values. When you see your values upheld in the world around you, you feel happy and satisfied. When your values are violated, you feel angry and frustrated.

Stress and unhappiness arise when you compromise your values in some part of your life. Most relationship problems revolve around a conflict of values. Happiness in relationships is the result of two or more people sharing the same values in the same order of importance. You can resolve most of your problems by returning to the values that are most important to you.

Your values are organized in a hierarchy. You have values that are higher than some and lower than others. You have a primary value, a secondary value, a tertiary value, and so on.

You demonstrate your values in your behaviors. It is not what you say but what you do that shows you and the world around you what you truly believe. A person cannot do one thing on the outside and be someone else on the inside.

You will always sacrifice a lower-order value in favor of a higher-order value when you are forced to choose between them. When you are under pressure, you reveal your true character. When you are under pressure, you will choose the value that is dearest to you. You demonstrate who you are on the inside when you are forced to make a choice on the outside.

For example, imagine two people with the same three values. These values are family, health, and career success. However, John's order of values is different from Jim's. John's primary value is his family. After his family comes his health, and after his health comes career success.

Jim has the same three values but in a different order. Jim values career success first, family second, and health third.

Is there a difference between John and Jim? Is there a small difference or a large difference? Which of the two people would you prefer to have as a friend? If you met the two people at a social occasion, would you be able to tell which person was which on the basis of their conversation and behavior?

The answer is clear. A person's choice of values determines his or her character and personality. In general, it determines his or her priorities and choices. It dictates his or her conversation and interests. A person's values determine what he or she will do and won't do. The order of a person's values is the critical factor in shaping his or her destiny.

Values are reflected in how people behave when they are forced to choose. Anyone can express high and noble values when nothing is at stake. But when there is a price to pay, a sacrifice to make, a discipline to adhere to, people reveal their true selves and their true beliefs.

Of course, as discussed in Chapter Two, tasks that are both urgent and important take highest priority. For example, a man who values his family above his career might choose to miss a family dinner if a very important meeting comes up; a woman who values her career above her health might take time off to deal with a pressing medical problem. Their values have not changed, but their actions reflect both the urgency and the importance of events in their lives.

You develop your values early in life as the result of the influences around you. If you grow up with good role models, you will develop life-enhancing values that help you to become a successful, happy person. If you grow up with no role models or receive no guidance in values, you can reach maturity and have little or nothing that you believe in or stand for.

Sometimes your values are called your *organizing principles*. These are the standards you use to judge your behavior and the behavior of others. These are the rules you follow when you make decisions. When you are clear about your values and their order of priority, you find it much easier to make decisions in the critical moments of your life.

One of my clients was a large conglomerate that was developing a telecommunications division. The first thing they did was to spend several weeks discussing their values and developing their mission statement for this new division. Once they had defined their values, they agreed on the meaning of those values and how those values would be used to guide behavior.

Whenever the managers or executives of the company had a question or a problem, they took out a laminated card describing their values and discussed the problem with the card in hand. They asked each other, "Based on this value, how should we handle this situation?" They then went through their values, using these definitions as the basis for discussion and decision making.

Interestingly enough, the company started with an idea and some seed capital in a highly competitive industry and became a great commercial success. The company continues to grow and is highly profitable. Everyone in the company knows and lives by the values. Everyone who works in the company is happy, enthusiastic, and highly motivated. Values make the difference.

. . . .

What are your values? What do you believe in? What do you stand for? What will you *not* stand for? What are your innermost convictions and your organizing principles? The accuracy with which you answer these questions will largely determine your happiness and your career success.

Review the list of values in the Appendix of this book and select the three to five values that best represent what you believe to be right and good and true about your work and your business. Some values you might choose for your career could be *integrity, dependability, quality, excellence, hard work*, and *customer service*. Examine your current behavior to determine how consistent it is with the values you espouse. Decide how you will behave in the future to ensure that your actions are consistent with the values you consider to be the most important.

Select one value that you feel is more important than any other value in your work life. Make this your focal point for your behavior and decision making. Resolve to be consistent with this value in everything you say or do. Never allow an exception. Let this value be your guiding light so that, years from now, people will still speak about you and this value in the same sentence.

Clarify Your Business and Career Vision

The second part of the Focal Point Process is to project forward and develop a clear vision of your ideal work life five years in the future. Imagine that, five years from now, everything is perfect and your work life is ideal in every way. Your vision must be consistent with your values. Answer these questions:

- What would your ideal job or position look like?

- What would you be doing most of the time?

- How much would you be earning?

- What kind of people would you be working with?

- What level of responsibility would you have?

- What kind of company or industry would you be working in?

- How would your colleagues and coworkers think and talk about you?

Practice back-from-the-future thinking. Project forward five years and then look back mentally to where you are today. Imagine the steps you would have had to take to make your future vision a reality. This exercise of projecting forward and then looking back to the present is extremely powerful in clarifying what you want and what you will have to do to achieve it.

What Is Your Mission?

Once you have a vision, the next step is to develop a mission for your career. A mission is an ideal description of what you want to accomplish in your career in the years ahead. A mission is something that is both achievable and measurable. A clear mission statement, revolving around your values, is such that an objective third party can tell you whether you have achieved the mission.

A mission statement can be very short and to the point. The mission statement for AT&T for many years was "Bring telephone access to every American." The mission statement for the Coca-Cola Company is "Beat Pepsi!" The mission statement for the Pepsi-Cola Company is "Beat Coke!"

Perhaps the most famous mission statement of the twentieth century was contained in the orders given by General George C. Marshall to General Dwight D. Eisenhower when he took command of the allied forces in World War II: "Proceed to London. Invade Europe. Defeat the Germans."

Your personal career mission statement might be something like this: "Based on my values of integrity, quality, and customer service, my mission is to take care of my customers better than anyone else. As a result, I will earn more than $100,000 per year and score consistently in the top 10 percent of people in my field."

What Is Your Purpose?

Your purpose for your career flows from your values, vision, and mission. Your purpose is the reason why you do what you do. It is the reason why you get up in the morning. Your purpose is the reason why you work at this particular job or in this particular industry in the first place. Your purpose is what gives meaning to your work and your life.

Both a mission and a purpose in your work are always defined in terms of improving and enhancing the life and work of other people in some way. Your mission and purpose are always defined in terms of external contribution. Your mission and purpose describe the difference you intend to make in the world as a result of who you are and what you do. They explain your value offering, both personally and as a business.

Once you have determined your values, vision, mission, and purpose, you organize your work life so that you live consistently with them every hour of every day. If you are truly living consistently with the very best that is in you, other people around you will know what your values, vision, mission, and purpose are without your having to tell them.

Here's a question. Based on your current behavior, if researchers were to ask your coworkers what they thought your values, vision, mission, and purpose were, what do you think they would say in response? In other words, how do you think other people think and talk about you when you are not there? How do the people who work with you and deal with you from day to day assess the quality of your character and the values you live by? These are some of the most important questions you can ever ask. And the answers should not be left to chance.

Set Goals for Your Business and Career

Your goals are the measurable objectives you must attain to fulfill your mission and purpose and realize your vision. They are the targets you aim at. What are your goals for your work and career?

Your goals must be clear, written, and specific. They must be believable and achievable. They must be accompanied by written plans and schedules for their accomplishment. You must work on them every day.

Each goal must include performance measures, or benchmarks. These numbers allow you to clearly determine whether you are moving closer to your goals or further away.

A performance measure is a key number of some kind that gives you an indication of performance or effectiveness in a particular area. In every part of your life, you need these measures to evaluate how well you are doing. Your measures serve as scorecards to indicate success or failure in your activities. The choice of a specific standard of performance becomes a primary focal point for your career.

One obvious measure, or focal point, is the amount you earn each year. Another is the rate of increase in your pay, year by year. A measure could be how often you have been promoted in the last two years. Another could be your percentile ranking in comparison with others in your field.

Many self-employed professionals use their hourly rate as the critical success factor by which they evaluate their performance and effectiveness. The amount they earn per hour, and how often they earn that amount, is a summary indicator of how well they are doing in many other parts of their careers.

What are your key standards of performance for your work? How do you measure your success on a day-to-day, week-to-week, month-to-month basis?

When you set clear goals for yourself, you should write them down, make plans to achieve them, and work on

them every day. Be sure that you have a clear measure of
your progress that you can refer to regularly. This becomes
your focal point. This is where you mark the "X" in your
work life.

Upgrade Your Business and Career Knowledge and Skills

What additional knowledge or skill will you need to achieve
your goals and fulfill your vision? Remember that if you're not
getting better, you're getting worse. What are the core competencies that you will have to develop if you want to lead your
field in the years ahead? How do you plan to acquire these
core competencies?

Four Keys to Career Success

There are four keys to success in making yourself more valuable, marketing yourself more effectively, and moving yourself
ahead more rapidly in your career: specialization, differentiation, segmentation, and concentration.

1. *Specialization* is your ability to channel your talents
and abilities into a vital area that is of measurable value to your
company or your customers. Your selection of an area of specialization is a critical determinant of your long-term success.
What is yours?

2. *Differentiation* is how you set yourself apart from others on the basis of your superior performance in one or more
areas. Your ability to differentiate yourself on the basis of high-
quality work probably is the most important single focal point
of your career. Just as a company must have an area of excel-

lence or competitive advantage to survive and thrive, you must have at least one as well. What is it?

If your customers and coworkers were asked, "What is his or her area of excellence?" what would they say about you? In what part of your work are you outstanding? What do you do better than anyone else? Where do you perform at a high level of effectiveness?

If you do not yet have an area of excellence, you must begin immediately to develop one. Consider both your abilities and your company's or your customers' needs. What should it be? What could it be? What is your plan to become outstanding at what you do? And how will you measure your level of excellence in a particular area of knowledge or skill? This measure becomes your standard of performance, your focal point. This is where you mark the "X" in your career. This is where you focus your attention.

Becoming excellent in a critical skill area can do more to advance you in your career than perhaps any other decision you make or action you take.

3. *Segmentation* is the ability to determine the people and organizations in your work life that can most benefit the fastest from your performance in a particular area. In segmentation, you define your most important customer clearly and then resolve to satisfy that particular customer better than anyone else.

Often, you can change the entire direction of your business or your career by changing the definition of the customer you are going to focus on in the future.

4. *Concentration* is your ability to focus single-mindedly on serving your specific market segment with products and services that are excellent for that individual or organization.

These four strategies—specialization, differentiation, segmentation, and concentration—are the essential focal points for achieving extraordinary results in your company and in your career.

Ask yourself, "What one skill, if you developed it and did it in an excellent fashion, would have the greatest positive impact on your career?" Whatever your answer to that question, write it down as a goal, set a deadline, make a plan, and begin working on developing yourself in that area until you master it. This is the real key to career success.

Develop Winning Business and Career Habits

First you shape your habits, and then your habits shape you. What specific habits of thought and action can help you to do your best and become excellent in your chosen field?

Developing new habits is an ongoing responsibility of adult life. It is too important to be left to chance. You must make it a matter of choice.

As it happens, everyone has habits. Unfortunately, many of these habits are bad ones, not particularly helpful or life enhancing, such as procrastinating or overeating.

Your job is to develop habits in each area of your life that make it progressively easier for you to do better and better in that area. And your habits are very much under your control.

Some of the habits of highly effective people are *punctuality*, *good time management*, *self-discipline*, *single-minded concentration*, *task completion*, and *thoughtfulness*. These are all habits you can develop, through repetition, that will help you to move ahead more rapidly. You are usually quite aware of the habits that would help you the most.

The good news is that any activity you repeat over and over eventually becomes a new habit. You can develop any habit that you consider desirable or necessary. By practicing a certain behavior until it becomes automatic, you can actually shape the development of your character and your personality.

There is a law of reversibility in psychology that is based on the "act as if" principle. William James of Harvard put it this way: "If you feel a certain way, you will act consistent with that feeling. But at the same time, if you *act as if* you already had the habit you desire, the action itself, repeated often enough, will develop within you the habit consistent with it."

To develop a habit you desire, you need only act on every occasion as if you *already* had the habit. By doing this, you will gradually develop the habit within yourself, action by action, until it becomes a permanent part of your personality. By taking control over the process of new habit pattern development, you take control over your future.

Your job is to select the one behavior that is consistent with the most important habit you could develop, put an "X" on that behavior, and practice it every single day until it becomes as natural to you as breathing.

Create Your Daily Business and Career Activity Schedule

The great wall that separates the successful person from the unsuccessful is action orientation. Talk is cheap; action is everything. Select the one activity you could do each day that would be the most helpful to you in achieving your most important goal. There is always one activity you could practice that is more valuable than anything else.

Keep yourself on track by asking continually, "What are my highest value activities? Why am I on the payroll? What exactly have I been hired to accomplish? What can I and only I do that, if done well, will make a real difference? What is the most valuable use of my time, right now?"

Use these questions as your focal points for achieving and maintaining high levels of performance and productivity.

Make Your Business and Career Action Commitment

The final element of the Focal Point Process, to ensure that you achieve your career goals, is your action commitment. What specific action are you going to take as a result of your answers to the questions in this chapter?

In the final analysis, a person who takes a single action as the result of a new idea or insight is far more valuable than the person who learns a hundred ideas but does nothing.

No-Limit Thinking

The opportunities and possibilities available to you in your career are almost without limit. There are more than 100,000 job categories in the United States alone, and this number is multiplying with every new increase of information and advance in technology.

There are no limits to what you can accomplish if you develop absolute clarity about who you are and what you want and then throw your whole heart into doing your job better than anyone else. This commitment will open up unlimited doors of opportunity for you.

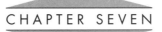

CHAPTER SEVEN

Improve Your Family and Personal Life

No success in public life can compensate for failure in the home.
—BENJAMIN DISRAELI

Happiness in life, in large measure, comes from good relationships with other people—in your family and your personal life as well as at your work. The work on emotional intelligence by Daniel Goleman and others suggests that your social skills will have more of an impact on your success than your intellectual ability, education, and experience combined.

You therefore owe it to yourself to become a relationship expert, to become very competent and capable in your interactions with others.

Fortunately, social skills are both learned and learnable. Within a wide range, you can develop the type of likable personality that will dramatically enhance the quality of your family and personal life.

In the Focal Point Process, you think through who you are and what is important to you with regard to other people. You then make clear decisions in specific areas, and you make action commitments based on these decisions. Thereafter, you discipline yourself to live consistently with the decisions and commitments you have made for yourself.

Determine Your Family and Personal Values

What are your values with regard to your family and other important people in your life? What are your unifying principles? What do you stand for in your relationships? What do you believe is proper behavior in your treatment of others? What do you feel is most important in the character and behavior of both you and others when dealing with other people?

When you are treating other people in a manner that reflects your highest values, you can feel it inside. You feel happier and more confident. You experience higher levels of self-esteem and self-respect. You feel greater peace and contentment within yourself. As a result, you live and work in greater harmony with the people around you. When you are living consistently with your values, every part of your personal life flows more smoothly.

Earlier I asked you to consider what you would do, how you would spend your time, if you found out today that you had only six months left to live.

Everyone who considers this question seems to answer it in very much the same way. They say that they would spend as much time as possible during that six months with the people they love and care about the most. All thoughts of material or financial goals seem to evaporate instantly when you know that you will not be around very much longer.

F. Scott Fitzgerald once wrote, "The mark of a first rate mind is the ability to hold two contradictory ideas at the same time and still retain the ability to function."

One of the exercises in Zen teaching is to envision living for a hundred years while contemplating dying within twenty-four hours. Your ability to hold these two thoughts simultaneously enables you to focus with greater clarity and calmness in the present moment.

The best way to live your life at home with your family is to balance the two thoughts, that of living for a long time and that of dying in the very near future. By holding these two thoughts in your mind simultaneously, you will treat people differently and better. This mental balancing act will immediately improve the quality of your relationships with the people closest to you.

Your values are expressed in your behaviors, especially when you are under pressure or exposed to temptation. When you are tired, irritable, stressed, afraid, or at a low point in your life, you often say and do things that are completely unexpected. You often express values and beliefs you did not know you had.

Select three to five values from the Appendix. Some values you might choose to guide your relationships could be *love*, *patience*, *kindness*, *sincerity*, *dependability*, *forgiveness*, *respect*, and *encouragement*.

If the members of your family were interviewed and asked how you truly felt about them, what would they say? From the way you treat them most of the time, what would your family members conclude about your fundamental values concerning them?

When I got married, I chose the value of *unconditional love* to be the organizing principle in all my family relationships. In more than twenty years of marriage, I have never deviated from that basic value with my wife and four children. If you were to ask any member of my family about my values regarding them, they would tell you that, whatever else, I love them unconditionally, 100 percent of the time, no matter what.

In addition, I practice truthfulness, dependability, respect, and patience. I am definitely not perfect, but my decision a long time ago to live by these values with my family has been one of the most important choices I ever made.

Choose the values you believe in the most strongly. Define those values in terms of the behaviors you would engage in to express those values. Resolve to treat all members of your family so that, at a later time, they could identify your values, even if you never told them what they were.

Above all, put an "X" on the most important of all your values, the one value that can have the greatest positive impact on your relationships. Hold fast to that value in all your interactions with the people close to you. Never deviate or compromise. Practice the value until it becomes automatic and easy. This can be one of the most important focal points in your life.

Clarify Your Family and Personal Vision

Project five years into the future. With your values clear, define your ideal vision for your personal and family life. Imagine that your personal life was perfect in every way. What would it look like? How would you feel about yourself and your significant others? What would you be doing each day? How would you and the people closest to you be living their lives?

Here are some questions for your back-from-the-future thinking:

■ What would be your perfect family lifestyle? If you could design a lifestyle that was perfect in every way, what would it look like?

■ What kind of a life and home environment would you want to provide or create for your family?

■ What kind of experiences would you want to enjoy in your family life? Imagine that you would have no limitations. Imagine that you could do anything at all with the people you love. What would you want to do differently from today?

■ What sort of items would you like to obtain for your family? What kind of material benefits would you like to provide for them?

■ How much time, how many days and weeks, would you like to spend with your family and friends each year, on long weekends and longer vacations?

■ What kind of a relationship would you like to have with each member of your family and those closest to you?

■ What sort of education or opportunities do you want to provide for your children?

■ If you were financially independent today, what changes would you make in your family and personal life?

■ What one great thing would you dare to dream for your family if you were completely guaranteed success?

Create a mission statement to guide and direct yourself and your family's behavior toward each other. It doesn't have to be complicated. A simple family mission statement could be something like this: "Our family mission is to create a loving environment where each person feels safe, respected, and free to develop his or her individual potential to become everything he or she is capable of becoming."

Your mission statement can be short or long, simple or complex. The main thing is that it is discussed, agreed upon, and shared by every member of your family. You then become responsible for repeating and reaffirming this mission statement on a regular basis. You must be a role model and live the mission statement in everything you say and do.

Select a focal point, a single repeated action or behavior you can practice consistently to demonstrate your commitment to the mission. This could be the practice of patience, listening, encouragement, or unconditional love. By emphasizing this behavior, you ensure that the other values are adhered to and the mission statement is followed.

Set Goals for Your Family and Personal Life

Decide specifically what you really want to achieve in your family life. This is a key part of the Focal Point Process. The clearer you are about the things you really want, the more rapidly you will bring them into your life. The happiest people spend a lot of time thinking about what they want to be, have, and do. As a result, their lives are far more interesting, exciting, and enjoyable than those of people who just drift along from day to day, with no clear idea of where they are going or why.

You can set both tangible and intangible goals for your family and other personal relationships. Tangible goals refer to homes, cars, bicycles, boats, clothes, and other physical objects. Tangible goals are important. You should give a lot of thought to the type of tangible goals you want for yourself and your loved ones.

Intangible goals are qualitative. They refer to time with your family and friends, vacations, walks, quality of life, health, the security of your home, and the well-being of each person. Intangible goals deal very much with the senses and the emotions and are therefore more important and immediate than tangible goals.

Remember that performance standards are measures you use to determine how close you are to achieving your various goals. If you can't measure it, you can't manage it or improve it. What gets measured gets done. The more specific you can be about the critical success factors in each part of your personal life, the more likely it is that you will make your personal life into something truly extraordinary.

Tangible Goals

Some of the tangible critical success factors you might use are the following:

■ What is the current size and layout of your home? Are you happy with this? Would you like to change it or improve it in some way? If so, how?

■ How satisfied are you with your household finances? What improvements would you like to make in the months and years ahead?

■ How secure is your family with regard to insurance? Do you have sufficient life insurance? Health insurance? Accident insurance? Car insurance? Disability insurance? What changes or additions should you make?

■ How prepared are you for education and college expenses for your children? How much will you need? What actions should you take today to start making proper provision for them?

■ Are you happy with the other material components of your life: your car, furniture, clothes, and appliances? What would you like to change, improve, or have more of?

Determine what you really want in each of these areas. Set each of them as a goal, make a plan, and go to work on your plan. Set standards or measures for each goal and then compare your progress against these measures on a regular basis. You will be amazed at how much you accomplish when you are clear about your targets and how you will measure your progress toward them.

Intangible Goals

Once you have set your tangible goals, you can set your intangible goals. These can be far more important than material goals that you can touch and measure.

Time is the critical success factor in all relationships. The quality of any relationship is directly related to the amount of time you invest in that relationship. You demonstrate a person's importance to you by spending time with him or her.

You can dramatically improve the quality of a relationship by investing more and more time in that relationship. This is the key intangible goal. Here are some questions for you:

■ How much time do you spend daily with your spouse or partner? How much time would you like to spend?

■ How much time do you spend daily with each of your children? How much time would you like to spend?

■ How much time do you spend daily with your friends? How much time would you like to spend?

■ How many days do you take off with your family or friends each week?

■ How many weekends away do you take with your spouse each year?

■ How many vacation weeks do you take with your family each year?

■ How often do you have dinner with your entire family?

■ How do you start each day with your family members?

■ What would you really like to have in your family or personal relationships that you don't currently have?

■ What grade would you give yourself on the quality of your communication with your loved ones? What grade would they give you?

■ If your family and personal life were ideal in every respect, how would things be different from what they are today?

In each case, determine how you could measure a change in your situation. What would have to happen? What would it look like? How could you tell that a change had taken place?

Select a single focal point and bring all your attention to bear on improving in that particular area. As you focus on one measurable change, improvements in other areas will start to take place almost immediately.

Upgrade Your Family and Personal Relationship Skills

Your life gets better only when you get better. What additional knowledge and skills will you need to improve the quality of your personal life? What subjects do you need to master so that you improve your relationships with your family and friends?

A few years ago, my wife, Barbara, and I decided to take up skiing so that we could have a focal point for our winter family vacations. It was a wonderful decision that has had an incredibly positive impact on our family life. It has given us something that we can all share in common.

Over the years, we have gone through the process of buying and upgrading ski clothes and equipment, year after year. Everyone in the family has learned to ski, and our children are accomplished snowboarders. The children have met new people on our ski vacations, and they have brought their friends along with them. The time away has enabled us to enjoy many hours of conversation and sharing that would not have been possible in the hustle and bustle of daily life, school, and work.

It is very easy to get into a rut in any area of life, including your family life. To counter this tendency, you should continually stretch beyond your comfort zone. Push yourself to do and try new things. Go to different places. Engage in new activities. Never allow yourself to become complacent or satisfied, doing the same old things year after year.

Develop Winning Family and Personal Relationship Habits

Think through and identify the additional habits and behaviors that will help you to enrich and improve the quality of your personal relationships. Perhaps you need to learn to listen better or to ask better questions. Perhaps you need to be more patient or more genuinely interested in the activities of your family and friends. Perhaps you need to develop the foresight and discipline to take time off from your work for family activities.

Select a specific habit or behavior that would be helpful for you to develop and put an "X" on that behavior.

Create Your Daily Family and Personal Activity Schedule

Choose specific things you can do each day to improve your personal relationships. Sometimes, small changes can make big differences.

Some of the most important and appreciated things you do for members of your family are things that they could easily do for themselves. Helping your loved ones with little tasks is a wonderful way for you to tell them how important they are to you.

Treating each member of your family as if he or she was the most important person in the world is a wonderful way to build their self-esteem and feelings of personal value. Telling them every day how much you love them can have a wonderful effect on their self-image and self-confidence.

Select a single daily activity that you are going to practice to improve your personal relationships. Then discipline yourself to engage in that activity repeatedly until it becomes a habit.

Four Key Questions

Here is an exercise for you. Sit down with your loved ones and ask them these four questions. Be ready for some interesting answers.

1. Is there anything I am doing today that you would like to me to do more of?

2. Is there anything I am doing that you would like me to do less of?

3. Is there anything I am not doing that you would like me to start doing from now on?

4. Is there anything I am doing that you would like me to stop doing?

You may be surprised at the answers you get in response to these questions. Whatever they say, resist the temptation to argue or defend. Listen quietly and attentively. Ask them for specific examples to help you understand. Thank them for their inputs and ideas. Take their answers away with you and turn them over slowly in your mind to evaluate them.

As a busy professional speaker, I travel and speak all over the country. Some years ago, I was often booked on a Saturday or Sunday on the East Coast and I ended up being away from home for as long as two weeks at a time.

Finally, my wife sat me down and told me that she did not want me working on the weekends any more. My first reaction was denial and disagreement. I argued and protested. I tried to explain how important it was that I continue to accept speaking engagements for whatever day of the week they were planned.

But as I thought it over, I realized that she was right. Being on the road and away from my family was distorting my priorities.

From that day forward, I refused to speak on weekends. Instead, I am home with my family almost every weekend. It has dramatically improved the quality of our family life, and it has not really hurt my business.

Good personal relationships are characterized by openness to input and ideas from each person. Keeping this in mind will make it much easier for you to make the adjustments necessary for happy, healthy relationships.

Building and Maintaining Good Relationships

Here are some ideas that can help you to enhance the quality of your family life:

■ Remember what is truly important in your life. Put your relationships ahead of all else. Make the needs of your loved ones the top priorities of your life. Make whatever adjustments or sacrifices in your work or external life are necessary to accommodate these relationships.

■ When you are at work, spend your time working. Don't waste time. Remember, any time you waste at work must eventually be taken away from your family when you bring work home.

■ Remember that there are two types of time spent in your life: There is work time, which is measured by results and productivity, and there is personal time, which is measured in terms of love and contentment.

The law says that *it is the quality of time at work that counts and the quantity of time at home that matters*.

By improving the quality of your work time, concentrating single-mindedly on your highest-value tasks and getting them done quickly and well, you can reduce the time you spend at work and increase the time available for your personal life.

At home, you need long, unbroken periods of time to build and maintain high-quality relationships. Love, affection, and trust building cannot be rushed. The more time you invest in relationships with the important people in your life, the higher quality of life you will have in all areas.

■ Remember that watching television, reading the newspaper, or working on your computer does not constitute spending time with your loved ones. Interacting, not just spending time in the same place, is what builds relationships.

■ Deliberately create chunks of time with your loved ones. Create thirty-, sixty-, and ninety-minute blocks of time where you can interact one-on-one and face-to-face.

Go shopping and go for walks with your family. Take long drives to a distant restaurant or to a resort with your spouse. And when you drive, leave the radio off. A car with no music playing is one of the greatest mobile communication chambers imaginable. You will be amazed at the wonderful conversations you can have in a quiet car.

■ Plan vacations in advance. Schedule them completely. Pay for them in full. Make the payments nonrefundable if possible. Then discipline yourself to take the time away, no matter what happens.

The times you spend away and on vacation with your loved ones will include the happiest and most important memories of your lives together. Your job is to create as many opportunities for these happy experiences to take place, and for these memories to develop, as you possibly can.

■ Remember that to do more of one thing, you must do less of another. To spend more time with your loved ones, you must do less of something else.

Before you commit to or engage in any behavior, ask yourself, "What will I have to *not* do in order to do this?" Compare the value of one activity with the other. Your ability to make good choices about how you spend your time largely determines the quality of your life.

Make Your Family and Personal Life Action Commitment

Make a specific action commitment based on what you have just read and the questions you have just answered. Do something. Do anything. But take action immediately to improve the quality of your personal relationships. Then, do something every day to move you toward the most important relationship goals you have set for yourself.

When you dedicate yourself to creating and maintaining a wonderful personal life, the quality of every other area of your life will improve. You will be happier, healthier, more rested, relaxed, and productive. You will experience greater happiness and satisfaction at home, and you will be far more effective and capable when you go back to work.

CHAPTER EIGHT

Achieve Financial Independence

Thought is the original source of all wealth, all success, all material gain, all great discoveries and inventions, and of all achievement.

—CLAUDE M. BRISTOL

One of my seminar participants once told me, "Money is like food. When you have enough of it, you don't think about it at all. But when you are deprived of it for any period of time, you think of nothing else."

Some people misquote the Bible by saying that money is the root of all evil. But the Bible actually says that *love* of money is the root of all evil.

However, it's more accurate to say that *lack* of money is the root of all evil. Very few problems are caused by having too much money. The problems that disrupt people's lives, health, and emotions are almost invariably caused by the fact that they have too little money.

We are living in the most prosperous age in human history. More people are achieving financial independence and becoming millionaires today, at a faster rate, than ever before. The majority of self-made millionaires and even self-made billionaires are first-generation success stories. They started their working lives with little or nothing and earned it all from the first dollar.

One of your primary responsibilities to yourself and the people in your life is to achieve financial independence, to reach the point where you never have to worry about money again. The fact that so many other people have gone from rags to riches in a single generation is ample proof that you can do it as well. You only need to learn how.

Making a million dollars is simpler than many people realize. If you simply saved $100 per month, year in and year out, from age 20 to age 65, and you invested that money in a well-managed mutual fund invested in the U.S. stock market, you would typically earn an average of 10.8 percent per annum on your investment. At that rate, $100 per month would be worth more than $1,200,000 when you retire.

So why doesn't everybody become a self-made millionaire over the course of his or her working life? There are three primary reasons. First, it never occurs to them that it is possible. It never dawns on them that they can do it if they really want to. As a result, they give up even before they start.

Second, if it does somehow occur to them that it is possible, they never make a firm, unequivocal decision to save and invest regularly throughout their working lives. They hope and wish and intend to start, but they never make the necessary decision that leads to action.

Third, if it does occur to them, and they do make such a decision, they procrastinate. They put off the beginning of a saving and investment program month after month and year after year until it is too late.

The most financially successful people in every society are those with a long time perspective. They develop a long time horizon. They think and plan ten, twenty, and even forty years into the future. They organize their daily and weekly activities in such a way that everything they do is consistent with the long-term goals they want to achieve. This is especially true with regard to financial independence.

Everyone, you included, has a series of goals, which may be clear or fuzzy. These goals are organized in a hierarchy. Each of your goals is ranked, consciously or unconsciously, from your most important to your least important. They are organized from your most intensely desired goals all the way down to your least desired goals, which you might like to achieve some-day but which don't really matter that much to you.

You can change your entire life by changing the order of priority and importance of your goals. The reason people do not achieve financial independence is because, although it is a goal, it is not a *primary* goal. It is merely one of many goals that they think about from time to time. When it comes time to act, their other goals take precedence.

It is only when you take the goal of financial independence and move it to the top of your hierarchy of values that you begin to get your financial life under control. As long as financial independence is jumbled up with all your other goals, you will never take the necessary actions to become wealthy.

Remember, you become what you think about most of the time.

In *The Millionaire Next Door*, Thomas Stanley cites the thousands of interviews that have led researchers to the discovery that self-made millionaires think about financial independence most of the time. They organize their lives around saving and accumulating. They think about how they can earn or acquire more and how they should invest and deploy their savings.

This does not mean that they are not family oriented. In fact, most self-made millionaires place family at the very top of their hierarchy of values. What this does mean is that savings, investments, careful spending, and frugality are central organizing principles of their financial lives.

In all probability, you are not going to win the lottery. No distant relative is going to die and leave you a lot of money. You are not going to discover gold or make a lucky hit in the stock market. The only way you are going to achieve financial independence is by saving and investing your money month after month, and year after year, until you have enough that you never have to worry about money again.

Determine Your Financial Values

Your values with regard to money are important motivational forces in your life. They determine your financial likes and dislikes, your decisions and actions, your emotions and responses. They affect every decision you make with regard to earning, saving, and investing. Your financial values are the critical drivers and determinants of everything you do with regard to money.

What are your personal values with regard to money? What does money mean to you? What do you think about people who are financially successful? What is your attitude toward wealth and affluence? In particular, what is your self-concept with regard to your ability to become financially successful yourself?

For most people, money means freedom, one of the highest of all human values. It means the ability to be and do what you want and to buy the things you need without worrying about the cost. Freedom is a powerful, driving force that has determined the course of history. Is this one of your values?

For many people, some of the values associated with money are security, independence, success, status, adventure, and even love, especially the love and respect of others. What are your values with regard to money?

Here is an important point. If you have negative values with regard to money, these values can sabotage you throughout your entire life. For example, if you think that having money is somehow wrong, or that people who are financially successful are somehow evil or dishonest, you will create a force field of negative energy around yourself that drives financial success away from you, no matter how hard you work to achieve it.

One of the smartest things you can do, for the rest of your life, is to admire, respect, and look up to people who have achieved financial success. This is because you always move in the direction of that which you most admire and respect. The more you admire and respect financial success, the more likely you are to do the same things financially successful people do. Eventually you will become the kind of person who achieves financial success yourself.

Clarify Your Financial Vision

What is your vision with regard to money and to your financial future? Project forward five years, ten years, twenty years into the future. Imagine that your financial life is perfect in every respect. Create a clear mental picture of your distant financial future as if your every financial dream had been realized. What does it look like?

How much would you like to be worth when you retire or stop working? What kind of lifestyle would you like to have at that time? How much will you have to save and invest every month, every year, to reach your long-term financial goals? These are questions most people seldom ask or answer.

Barbara D'Angelis asks this wonderful question: "When will you know that you have enough, and what will you do then?"

Imagine that you have no limitations on your long-term ability to achieve financial independence. Imagine that you have all the time and all the resources you need. Imagine that you have all the knowledge and all the experience you need. Imagine that you have all the contacts and all the opportunities you could ask for. If you could design your financial life to be perfect in every way, what would it look like?

Imagine that you have achieved a net worth of $10 million. What would you do, how would you change your life if you were completely independent financially? Make up a dream list of every single thing you would want in your life, tangible and intangible, if you had all the money you would ever need.

The greater clarity you have regarding your long-term financial future, the faster you will attract the people and resources that you will need to achieve it in your life and the more rapidly you will realize your vision.

Set Goals for Your Finances

What are your financial goals? Among your financial goals, which of them are most important? What is your financial focal point? Where do you draw the "X" in your financial life?

In general, you should have four financial goals: earn as much as you can, spend as little as you can, save and invest as much as possible, and protect yourself against unexpected reversals and lawsuits. Achieving each of these goals is very much under your control. They are matters of personal decision and design, not chance.

Questions for Creating Your Financial Future

- How much do you want to earn this year?

- How much do you want to earn next year?

- How much do you want to be earning five years from today?

- What is your plan to earn these amounts of money?

- How much do you want to be worth when you retire?

- How much will you have to save and invest each year to achieve that financial goal?

- What is your plan to acquire that amount of money?

- What do you need to do first? What do you need to do second?

- What do you need to do every day, every week, every month to achieve your long-term financial goals?

- Where do you draw the "X" in your financial life? What is your focal point?

There are certain measures you can use to determine how well you are doing. The greater clarity you have with regard to the measures you use, the more likely it is that you will achieve your long-term goals on schedule.

To begin, calculate your financial net worth today. Add up all your assets at market value and then subtract all your debts and liabilities. Determine your dollar value today, if you had to sell out everything you own and turn it into cash. This can be an eye-opening experience.

- What amounts do you currently save and invest each month?

- What percentage of your income do you put away?

- What are your monthly costs of living?

- What are your annual costs of living?

- How many years have you been working, and how much, on average, have you managed to accumulate each year?

Perhaps the best measure you can use, if financial independence is your goal, is to determine how much money you will need each month, each year, to live comfortably and then calculate how long you could sustain your current lifestyle on your current savings. This is called your *run rate*, or *burn rate*. This is a calculation of how long you can survive with what you have accumulated up to now. This is the best measure of your overall financial health.

Most people have a burn rate of less than a month. Many high-income people are only two months away from homelessness. They spend everything they make and a little bit more besides. If their incomes were cut off for any period of time, they would be in desperate straits.

Set clear financial goals and targets for each part of your financial life, both for the short term and for the long term. Examine every expenditure in your life and look for ways to reduce your monthly living costs. Set a goal to cut your expenses by 10 or 20 percent over the next ninety days. Make cost control and cost cutting a regular part of your life, no matter how much you earn.

Upgrade Your Financial Knowledge and Skills

What additional knowledge and skills do you need to achieve your financial goals? What skills and abilities do you need to earn the highest income possible for you and eventually achieve financial independence? The subject of money is complex, but you must master it if you are truly serious about getting your financial life under control.

The average self-made millionaire spends twenty to thirty hours each month studying the subject of money and carefully managing his or her finances. On the other hand, the average person spends only about a tenth of that amount of time per month thinking about his or her financial future, mostly paying bills and balancing the checkbook. Because you become what you think about most of the time, the more time you spend thinking about your money, the better you will become at managing it.

The first knowledge you will need to achieve financial independence is the knowledge of exactly how much you are earning today, how much you are spending each month, and how much you are worth.

To get your financial affairs under control, you must begin by carefully studying and evaluating each expenditure before you make it. You should keep a list of every dollar you spend and analyze your list regularly. The more attention you pay to your day-to-day spending, the smarter you will become about the amount of money flowing through your fingers.

Break the Law

Parkinson's law says that expenditures invariably rise to meet income. The more you earn, the more you spend. Even if you double or triple your income, you will eventually double or triple your expenses and end up no further ahead.

Financial success comes from breaking Parkinson's law. Financial success is possible only when you refuse to allow your expenditures to increase at the same rate that your income increases.

Here is a rule that will almost guarantee that you become wealthy over the course of your working lifetime: Save and invest 50 percent of any increase you earn in your salary or compensation for the rest of your career.

You can spend the other 50 percent of the increase on improving your standard of living. But resolve today to save half of every increase for the rest of your career. This discipline alone will ensure that you achieve financial independence, probably several years before you expect.

Here is a simple five-word formula for financial success: Spend less than you earn. Spend less than you earn and then save or invest the balance. This formula can make you rich.

Money Skills Are Learnable

Identify the specific skills you will need to develop to achieve financial independence. One skill you need is a solid knowledge of money and finances. You should read the best books and magazines on the subject. Attend good seminars on financial planning. Seek advice from others who are financially successful. Learn everything you can about how money is acquired, accumulated, and protected. Leave nothing to chance.

Above all, examine your work activities carefully and determine exactly what you do that pays you the most money. Apply the 80/20 Rule to your job every day. Identify the 20 percent of your tasks that account for 80 percent of the value of everything you do. Resolve to focus more and more of your attention on becoming better and better at the few activities that are worth more than all the rest.

Financial success comes from value creation. You create value in the work you do. You create value in the products and services you produce and sell in conjunction with others. The more value you add, the greater will be your own personal value and the higher will be the rewards you receive.

Every day, you must look for ways to add even more value than before. You must always seek ways to serve your company and your customers better, faster, cheaper, and more conveniently.

Develop Winning Financial Habits

There are certain habits and behaviors that lead inevitably to financial success. The first and most important habit is for you to pay yourself first. As George Clason wrote in his classic, *The Richest Man in Babylon,* "A part of all you earn is yours to keep."

Pay yourself first, off the top. Your goal is to eventually save 10 to 20 percent of your income throughout your life. Your aim should be to put this amount away regularly, to invest it with experts and to let it grow over time.

If you cannot afford to save 10 percent of your income, begin by saving 1 percent of your income. Begin saving and investing, even before you pay off your debts. Begin putting money away before you pay down the amounts you owe. This is very important.

By developing the habit of saving a certain percentage of what you earn off the top of every single paycheck, you will eventually change your entire attitude toward yourself and money. In a very short time, you will become comfortable living on the percentage you still have to spend. Meanwhile, you will find yourself paying off your debts, one after another. In a year or two, you will be out of debt and you will have a rapidly growing bank account and investment portfolio.

The key to long-term financial success in the stock market has always been based on the twin miracles of compound interest and dollar cost averaging. Albert Einstein called compound interest the eighth wonder of the world. If you put a little money away and let it grow month after month and year after year, it eventually grows into an enormous amount.

Dollar cost averaging in the stock market means that you invest a specific amount every month, year in and year out. Sometimes you invest at the top of the market, and sometimes you invest at the bottom. But your average cost of stocks ends up being lower and your growth rate is higher and more predictable than if you always tried to buy at the right moment.

Peter Lynch, successful manager of the Fidelity Magellan Mutual Fund, wrote, "It is not *timing* the market, but *time in* the market that determines long term success."

The most important habit you can develop to achieve financial independence is the habit of frugality. Carefully consider every expense before you make it. If possible, delay a large purchase for a day, a week, a month, or even longer. Take that time to think about it before you commit. When you put off a major purchase decision for any period of time, you often end up not making it at all.

Perhaps the most helpful habit of all is to learn to enjoy the act of saving and investing. Most people associate saving with sacrifice, pain, restriction, and deprivation. This is why most people do not save. They have the wrong mindset.

Financially successful people enjoy the act of saving and investing. It makes them happy to refrain from spending and instead put their money away for the long term. They enjoy the growing sense of financial freedom that regular saving gives them.

When you begin to look forward to every opportunity to put money away, you change your entire attitude toward money and investments. You begin to get tremendous pleasure and satisfaction from seeing your savings and investments grow over time.

Create Your Daily Financial Activity Schedule

There are four activities you should engage in every single day to achieve financial independence.

1. Carefully evaluate every expenditure before you make it. Delay every expenditure that you possibly can. Put it off until later, if you make it at all.

2. Set clear goals and targets for the amounts you intend to earn and keep. Measure your results against these targets every week and every month. What gets measured gets done.

3. Look for ways to reduce your monthly expenditures and instead save the money. Cut out all nonessential expenses. Keep asking yourself, "Do I really need this?" Resolve to reduce your monthly costs of living by as much as you can as quickly as possible. Every dollar you can save from your monthly expenses is an additional dollar that you can put into your financial freedom account.

4. Take every possible opportunity to increase your value or earning ability. Look for ways to upgrade your knowledge and skills. Concentrate on getting better at the activities that contribute the greatest value to you and your company. Focus on making more and saving more every single day.

Make Your Financial Action Commitment

Select at least one action that you can take immediately that will begin moving you toward financial independence.

This activity can be as simple as opening up a separate bank account into which you deposit a specific percentage of every single paycheck from now on. It can be as complex as sitting down and drawing up a complete financial plan for your life.

Financial success is predictable. It has never been more possible for you to earn and keep more money than it is today. There are hundreds of thousands of self-made millionaires, all of whom started with nothing and who began using the practices and processes described in this chapter. If your goal is to become one of them, begin today.

CHAPTER NINE

Enjoy Superb Health and Fitness

Thoughts lead on to purposes; purposes go forth in action; actions form habits; habits decide character; and character fixes our destiny.

—TRYON EDWARDS

R esolve today that you are going to live to be eighty or ninety years old. Decide that you are going to dance at your grandchildren's weddings and that you are going to feel terrific about yourself all the days of your life, from this moment onward.

This is the most wonderful time in human history to be alive in terms of health and longevity. It has never been more possible for you to live longer and live better than today.

In 1901, the average life span was less than fifty years. In 2001, the average life span is seventy-seven years and increasing every year. One of the fastest-growing population groups in our society is people who are more than eighty, ninety, and even a hundred years old. Your goal should be to live as long as they do.

Your future intentions, your long-term visions and goals, have an inordinate impact on your present decisions and actions. Sometimes I ask my seminar audiences, "How many of you have decided how long you intend to live?"

Most people are surprised at the question. In general, people do not like to think too much about the fact that they will not live forever, so they put off thinking about a long life at all. When I ask this question, most people respond with a combination of confusion and discomfort.

However, if you say that you want to live to be eighty, you now have a focal point. You have a place where you can put the "X" in your life. You can now examine every single part of your physical life to determine whether the way you are living is likely to get you to age eighty.

One of the smartest things you can do, right now, is to stop doing anything that may interfere with your living a long, healthy life. If you stop doing certain things that are harmful and start doing other things that are helpful, you can change your health dramatically in a very short time.

Remember that there are four ways to change: You can do more of some things, you can do less of other things, you can start doing something that you have not done before, and you can stop doing something that is not helpful to you or to achieving your goals.

In the long run, you are free to choose what you do or what you don't do. You are in control. You are responsible. In terms of your physical health, you are where you are and what you are largely because of decisions you've made.

Determine Your Health and Fitness Values

What are your values with regard to physical fitness and well-being? How important is physical health to you? How high does it rank in your hierarchy of importance? How do you think about physical well-being, and how often do you think that way?

You become what you think about most of the time. People who are fit and healthy think about fitness and health most of the time. They think about physical well-being morning, noon, and night. They organize their entire lives around the specific behaviors and activities that will ensure that they live a long, happy life. And so should you.

Good health is something most people take for granted until they are deprived of it. Most people do not think about their health at all until they have an illness or an accident that forces them to think about their health almost exclusively.

Start by clarifying your values in this area. Some of the values associated with health and fitness are happiness, energy, beauty, discipline, self-control, personal mastery, persistence, and fitness. Which of these values most appeal to you? Select three to five values from the Appendix and organize them in your own personal order of priority.

Which value is most important to you? Which comes second? Which comes third? And so on. Motivation requires motive, and the clearer you are about your values regarding your health and well-being, the easier it is for you to make the decisions and sacrifices necessary to have a long, happy life.

Clarify Your Health and Fitness Vision

What is your long-term vision for your health? Project five or ten years into the future. If your health were perfect in every respect, what would you look like? How would you feel?

Make out a dream list. Describe your perfect self and lifestyle in terms of health and fitness. How much would you weigh? How much would you exercise? How many hours per night would you sleep? What time would you go to bed, and what time would you get up? What sort of physical activities would you engage in regularly? If your physical life were perfect in every respect, what would you be doing and how would you be doing it?

Set Goals for Your Health and Fitness

Set specific goals for your desired levels of physical fitness, health, and well-being. To set proper goals, you must select the critical success factors or measures that are associated with health and fitness. Do a complete analysis of yourself at the current time. Be perfectly honest with yourself. Create a baseline that you can compare your progress against. Ask yourself the following questions:

- How much do you weigh?

- How many hours per night do you sleep?

- What is your waist size?

- How often do you exercise each week?

- How many minutes per week do you exercise?

- How much do you eat?

- How nutritious is your diet?

- How much alcohol do you drink daily and weekly?

- What time do you go to bed at night? What time do you get up in the morning?

- How would you rate your health overall, on a scale of 1 to 10?

Any one of these measures can be the focal point for your goal of achieving superb levels of health and fitness. For myself, I have determined that my waist size is where I put the "X" in my life. Everything I do, or fail to do, with regard to diet, exercise, sleep, and overall fitness can be easily measured by the size of my waist at any given time. This is my personal focal point because it gives me a quick measure of success in every other area. What is yours?

Upgrade Your Health and Fitness Knowledge and Skills

Identify the knowledge and skills you will need to achieve and maintain superb physical health. The reason most people do not learn and grow in a given area is that they assume that they already know everything they need to know. They make the dangerous assumption that their personal knowledge is all the knowledge that exists on a particular subject. As a result, they make no effort to learn and apply anything new. This attitude makes it impossible for them to learn and grow.

One of the smartest things you can do is begin with the assumption that there is a lot you don't know in an important area of your life. Assume for a moment that much of what you know is inaccurate or incomplete. Become a student. Be like a child, open to all kinds of ideas, information, and influences. Approach the area of health and fitness as though there have been incredible breakthroughs in knowledge, which is true, and that any one of these great ideas can have an inordinate impact on how long you live and how good you feel about yourself.

For example, I received a letter recently from one of my seminar graduates. He had changed his career, upgraded his skills, tripled his income, and become a millionaire in less than ten years. But he had been unsuccessful in getting rid of about 20 pounds of excess weight.

Then one day, while he was listening to one of my audio programs, he heard me explain the importance of eliminating the white flour, sugar, and salt from one's diet. This had never occurred to him before, so he decided to give it a try.

In less than five months, he dropped the 20 pounds. He wrote and told me that this weight loss had transformed his life. He felt better about himself, had more energy, and slept better at night. He looked better and felt more effective and confident in his work and in all his interactions with other people. He was both amazed and delighted that a single piece of information had enabled him to achieve a health goal he had had for almost ten years.

There are physical fitness and health skills you can learn to ensure that you live a long, lean, healthy, and fit life. There are thousands of books and articles on the subject. You can join a health club and begin a physical fitness program. You can take yoga lessons and learn how to stretch your body and improve your overall health. You can learn aerobics or practice some other physical fitness routine. You can learn a new sport or begin jogging or swimming. You can take nutrition and cooking classes at a local clinic or school.

In every case, you should assume that there are wonderful ideas and methods available that can help you dramatically improve your health and well-being. Become a lifelong student of the best ideas for long life.

Develop Winning Health and Fitness Habits

Developing new habits and behaviors is central to the Focal Point Process. To achieve superb physical and mental health, there are specific things you can do every single day to promote long life and happiness. Your goal is to learn and practice them until they become automatic.

The good news is that tens of thousands of men and women have been interviewed and observed over ten, twenty, and thirty years to determine exactly what behaviors lead to the highest levels of health and well-being. Now we know what to do and what not to do.

Seven Secrets of Superb Health

The first secret of health, happiness, and long life is to *achieve and maintain proper weight*. Your doctor can help you determine your ideal weight, or you can get a more general idea from height and weight charts. Being overweight is a major health problem. More than 50 million Americans are officially classified as obese. This means that they are more than 20 percent above their ideal weight.

There is a simple five-word formula for weight control: Eat less and exercise more.

I ran into a friend recently who had lost more than 30 pounds after being overweight for several years. I asked him his secret. He said to me, with a big smile, "I made an amazing discovery. I found that I never gained weight from anything that I didn't eat."

Hundreds of thousands of people lose weight and keep it off every year. So can you. Set your ideal weight as a goal, make a plan, and work on your plan every single day. Do not deviate from your plan or allow exceptions until you achieve your ideal weight. Then dedicate yourself to staying at your ideal weight for the rest of your life.

The second secret of superb health is to *eat a proper diet*. When researchers examined the diets of Olympic athletes from more than 120 countries, they found that these high-performance diets all had three things in common:

- The athletes ate a wide variety of foods to receive a full spectrum of nutrients.

- They ate a lot of lean-source protein. This is protein that is low in fat, such as fish, chicken, and high-quality beef or pork. Some of them were vegetarians who ate soy-based foods, but they all avoided fatty foods.

- They drank lots of water. You need about 1 gallon of water per day to flush toxins from your body and keep it functioning at its best.

The key to an excellent diet is fairly simple. Eat more fruits and vegetables. Eat lean-source proteins. Eat lots of whole-grain products, such as whole wheat bread and bran muffins. Drink lots of water, at least one 8-ounce glass per hour. And avoid sugar, salt, and white flour products.

The third secret of superb health is proper *exercise*. Ideally, you should exercise and articulate every joint in your body every single day, even if you only take a few minutes in the morning to stretch and warm up your muscles. You should exercise three to five times each week, thirty to sixty minutes each time. One of the best focal points for physical health is to set a goal to exercise 200 to 300 minutes each week. You then carefully track the number of minutes you exercise each day to be sure you hit your target.

You can get your 200 to 300 minutes of exercise each week by walking, bicycling, jogging, swimming, or working out with various types of equipment at home or at a gym. You can get your quota of hours and minutes on a treadmill or a stationary bike.

Many people say that they don't have time to exercise regularly. However, studies show that the more physical exercise you engage in on a daily and weekly basis, the more energy you have. The more you exercise, the less sleep you need, the brighter and sharper you are when you work, and the more productive you are at everything you do. Investing time in regular exercise pays off in improved performance and longer life.

The fourth secret of superb health is *proper rest and relaxation*. It shouldn't surprise you to learn that most working people are getting too little sleep and functioning in a fog each day. You need seven to eight hours of sleep per night to function at your very best. In times of stress and overwork, you need even more. Don't shortchange yourself.

Take at least one full day off from work each week. On this day, you discipline yourself to do absolutely nothing associated with work. Relax completely. Refuse to read, make phone calls, work on your computer, or catch up with your assignments or responsibilities. Instead, go for a walk, watch television, go to a movie, or go out to dinner. But don't do any work at all for at least one day per week.

Take minivacations of two or three days as often as you can, once per month if possible. During this time, refuse to take any work with you. Just relax, exercise, sleep, and spend time with the important people in your life.

In addition, you should take one-, two-, and three-week vacations every year, during which you do nothing but rest and rejuvenate. The more rested you are, the brighter, sharper, more alert, and more productive you will be at your work and in every other area of your life. You will get more done by taking more time off.

The fifth secret of superb health is to *take proper nutritional and dietary supplements*. I began studying nutrition when I was twenty-one years old. I was amazed to discover that most of the foods we eat today do not include sufficient vitamins, minerals, and trace elements for maximum performance.

Some people say you can get all the nutrients you need if you simply eat a balanced diet. But the experts claim that you would need to eat as much as 20 pounds of food each day to get all the nutrients you need for optimal health.

Discuss nutrition and supplements with your doctor. Do your homework. Read about health and nutrition. Take balanced vitamin and mineral supplements. Sometimes, if your body needs it, adding a single ingredient such as iron, selenium, or chromium can have a transforming effect on your overall feelings of health and well-being.

The finest vitamin and mineral supplements ever, developed by the most advanced biochemists and nutritional experts, are now available from a variety of sources. Do your research, select the very best combination for you, and begin taking the supplements you need to perform at your best.

The sixth secret of superb health is to *stop smoking*. Smoking is probably the worst thing you can do to your body. Smoking has been associated with thirty-two different illnesses, ranging from cancers of the nose, throat, larynx, lungs, esophagus, and stomach to arterial sclerosis, heart disease, diminished brain functioning, osteoporosis, and gingivitis, a deterioration of the gum tissue that leads to foul breath and rotten teeth.

The seventh secret of superb health is to *reduce or eliminate alcohol consumption.* An enormous number of physical, mental, and social problems are caused by excessive alcohol consumption: family arguments, traffic accidents, cirrhosis of the liver, brain damage, and a variety of other physical problems.

The ancient Greeks had a saying: "Moderation in all things." This is a wonderful piece of advice not only for alcohol consumption but for every other part of your physical health regimen.

Create Your Daily Health and Fitness Activity Schedule

Choose the daily activities you are going to engage in to achieve and maintain high levels of physical health and well-being. Write them down; make a schedule and a plan. Put health and fitness into your daily agenda, just as you would an appointment with an important client. Move health and fitness activities to a higher level on your hierarchy of values and goals. Put other activities aside and put off lower-value tasks so that you have more time to take care of yourself. This is one area where you should never procrastinate or delay.

Make Your Health and Fitness
Action Commitment

What one action commitment are you going to make today to begin moving toward superb levels of physical well-being? Whatever it is, resolve to do it now. Start the game. Put the ball in play. Launch a lifetime program of healthy living and physical fitness.

CHAPTER TEN

Become Everything You Are Capable of Becoming

*The potential of the average person is like a huge ocean unsailed,
a new continent unexplored, a world of possibilities waiting to
be released and channeled toward some great good.*

—BRIAN TRACY

My first job after leaving school without graduating was washing dishes in the kitchen of a small hotel. This was the first of a series of laboring jobs—stacking lumber in a sawmill, digging wells, working on farms and ranches, putting nuts on bolts on a factory production line—that occupied me for the first few years of my career.

The turning point in my life came when I discovered the law of cause and effect, the great law of the universe and human destiny. I learned that everything happens for a reason. I discovered that success is not an accident. Failure is not an accident, either. I also discovered that people who are successful in any area usually are those who have learned the cause-and-effect relationship between what they want and how to get it. They then did repeatedly what other successful people did in a particular area until they got the same results. This insight changed my life.

No one is better than you and no one is smarter than you. They may be better or smarter in different ways, at least for the present. If someone is doing better than you are today, it is probably because he or she has discovered the cause-and-effect relationship before you have. And anything anyone else has done, within limits, you can do as well. The fact that someone else has achieved a worthy goal is the very best evidence that you can achieve that goal too.

Many people delude themselves into thinking that they can do what failures do and somehow, by some miracle, get the results successful people get. Even worse, they think they can do little or nothing at all and by some great stroke of luck, all their problems will be solved and their dreams will come true. But this is not the way the world works.

Wolfgang von Goethe once wrote, "To have more, you must first be more." To achieve more in your outer world, you must go to work on your inner world, on developing yourself. There are no lasting shortcuts. There is no other way.

Personal and professional development is the most powerful tool you can use to achieve any goal you set for yourself. You can move yourself from wherever you are to wherever you want to go by learning how others have done it before you and then by following the paths they have already blazed.

It is often said that the average person uses only 10 percent of his or her potential. According to studies done at the Stanford University Brain Institute, however, it is actually closer to 2 percent. On average, people have enormous reserves of potential that they habitually fail to use. Nature is exceedingly generous. It provides each person with an abundance of abilities and possibilities, most of which go untapped throughout life.

If you were to use only a small additional percentage of your inborn capabilities, you could probably double or triple your results. You could accomplish things far beyond anything you have ever done up to now. You could be healthier, happier, and more prosperous than you have ever imagined.

Abraham Maslow said that the story of the human race is the story of men and women "selling themselves short." Most people settle for far less than they are truly capable of. Most people create all kinds of justifications and rationalizations for poor performance. They convince themselves or allow themselves to be convinced, on the flimsiest evidence, that they lack the potential and ability of other people who are doing better than they are. They settle for a mediocre existence rather than committing themselves to breaking their own mental shackles and escaping from their own mental prisons.

When you see a person like Arnold Schwarzenegger, you do not dismiss his muscular development by attributing it to luck or genetics. You know that he has worked for many years and invested thousands of hours to develop himself physically.

But everyone starts with pretty much the same muscular structure Arnold Schwarzenegger started out with as a skinny teenager growing up near Graz, Austria. The only difference is that Arnold Schwarzenegger has developed his muscles and the average person has not.

In terms of mental ability and potential, most people are quite similar. Everyone has the same brain structure. Everyone has a variety of talents and abilities. Some people start off with greater natural advantages and personal endowments, but on average, each person has the ability to develop far beyond anything he or she has achieved so far.

Determine Your Personal Growth and Development Values

To realize your full potential for personal and professional growth and development, begin with your values as they apply to your own abilities. As you know, your values are expressed in your words and actions. You can tell what your values are by looking at what you do and how you respond to the world around you. Your values are the root causes of your motivations and your behaviors.

Some things you might value with regard to your personal growth are excellence, self-actualization, education, skill, achievement, and personal mastery. My primary value, in terms of personal development, can be summarized as *realizing my full potential*.

I believe that each person has the potential to do something wonderful with his or her life. I believe that within every person there is a giant waiting to come out. I believe that each person can do much more than he or she has ever done before, if only he or she learns how. That is my fundamental value. What is yours?

Clarify Your Personal Growth and Development Vision

Create a long-term vision for yourself in the area of personal growth. Project forward five or ten years and imagine that you are developed fully in every important part of your life. Idealize and see yourself as outstanding in every respect. Refuse to compromise on your personal dreams.

What level of skill or ability would you have in your field? What level of status and prestige would you have attained as the result of your superb performance at what you do? What kind of work would you be doing, and at what level would you be doing this work? How would you think and feel about yourself as the result of being one of the very best at what you do? If you had no limitations at all, what would be your vision for how you would develop yourself in the months and years ahead?

Set Goals for Your Personal Growth and Development

Now take your vision and crystallize it into specific goals. Here is a good way to start. Take out a piece of paper and write down ten goals that you would like to achieve in the area of personal and professional development in the months and years ahead. Write in the present tense, exactly as if you were already the person you intend to be. Determine exactly what you want to be able to do. Decide who you want to become. Describe exactly what you will look like when you become truly excellent in your field and in your personal life.

Then review this list of ten goals and select the one goal that, if you achieved it, would have the greatest positive impact on your life and on your career. Put a circle around that goal and move that goal to a clean sheet of paper.

Create a schedule for achieving this goal. Set deadlines for achieving certain benchmarks. Set subdeadlines as well.

Make a list of everything you can think of that you will have to do to achieve personal excellence in that area. Organize your list into a plan by setting priorities for each of the items. Gather the books, materials, equipment, and other resources you will need to begin work on yourself and your goal.

Take immediate action on at least one item in your plan to get the process started. Resolve to do something every day until you are successful in that area. Never stop working on yourself until you become the kind of person you would ideally most like to be.

When he was just starting out, actor Jim Carrey had a vision and a goal to be paid $10 million for acting in a movie. He made out a check to himself for this amount and carried it with him everywhere. He looked at it continually and never stopped believing in his ability to earn $10 million for a single picture.

Recognizing and believing in his talent, however, was not enough. He worked on his craft. He took every role he could possibly get and threw his whole heart into performing that role the very best he possibly could. He developed his ability to speak, to dramatize, and to entertain. He continually stretched his own envelope of performance. He took every lesson he could take and studied every element of professional acting he could learn from the people around him.

After years of hard work, his dream finally came true. He received $10 million for his role as the Joker in *Batman Forever*. Before he was forty, he was earning $20 million per film.

He makes one or two movies each year. He is now one of the most successful actors in Hollywood, if not in the world, because he had a clear vision and a dream and he never lost sight of it. Most important, he continued to work on himself and his craft until he was the kind of performer who was worth $20 million per picture.

Upgrade Your Personal Knowledge and Skills

Set specific measures for each of your goals. If your goal is to excel in your field, determine how you will know when you have achieved it. Decide how you can measure your progress and evaluate your success. Perhaps you can use as a measure the number of hours you study in your field each week. Perhaps you can measure the number of books you read or the number of audio programs you listen to. Perhaps you can measure your progress by the number of appointments you get or the number of sales you make as the result of your growing skills.

Compare yourself against these measures regularly. The more precise your measures and the more you pay attention to them, the better you will become in that area and the greater progress you will make.

Here are some key goal questions you can ask and answer for yourself:

■ What additional knowledge do you need to be the best in your field?

■ What additional skills must you acquire to do your work in an excellent fashion?

- What subjects do you need to study and master?

- What skills can you improve that will help you the most in your work or career?

- What are the key result areas of your job? What must you be excellent at doing to lead in your field?

- What are your core competencies today, and what new competencies must you develop to excel in your field in the future?

- What is your plan to excel in each of these areas?

- What is your plan to acquire these critical skills?

- What one skill or ability, developed and done in an excellent fashion, would have the greatest positive impact on your life and your career?

You first determine your values, your vision, your goals, and the knowledge and skill you will need to achieve them. You choose the ways in which you will measure your progress toward each of them. You then do something every day that makes you better in some way. You read, take courses, listen to audio programs, practice your new skills, and never stop improving.

Develop Winning Personal Growth and Development Habits

Select the specific habits and behaviors you will need to practice every day to become the person you want to become. These could be the habits of clarity, planning, thoroughness, studiousness, hard work, determination, and persistence.

Perhaps the most important single quality for success is self-discipline. Twentieth-century thinker-writer Elbert Hubbard defined self-discipline as "the ability to make yourself do what you should do, when you should do it, whether you feel like it or not."

Napoleon Hill of *Think and Grow Rich* fame called self-discipline "the master key to riches."

Every day, and every hour of every day, you have to practice self-discipline. You have to command yourself to do what is right, necessary, and important, or you will end up doing what is fun, easy, and unimportant. Self-discipline is the quality that enables you to choose to do the most important task, whether you feel like it or not, and stick to it. Self-discipline is an indispensable quality of all high-performing men and women.

Create Your Daily Personal Growth and Development Activity Schedule

There are seven disciplines you must develop if you want to achieve all that is possible for you. You can learn these disciplines through practice and repetition until they become automatic.

1. *Daily goal setting:* Every morning, take three to five minutes to write out your top ten goals in the present tense. Get a spiral notebook for this purpose. By writing out your ten goals at the beginning of each day, you will program them deep into your subconscious mind. This daily goal writing will activate your mental powers. It will stimulate your mind and make you more alert. Throughout the day, you will see opportunities and possibilities to move more rapidly toward your goals.

2. *Daily planning and organizing:* Take a few minutes, preferably the night before, to plan out every activity of the coming day. Always work from a list. Always think on paper. This is one of the most powerful and important disciplines of all for high performance.

3. *Daily priority setting:* The essence of all time management, personal management, and life management is contained in your ability to set the proper priorities on the use of your time. You use the methods described in Chapter Two to select the most valuable and important task you could possibly do and start work immediately on that task. This is essential for high performance.

4. *Daily concentration on your highest-value activities:* Your ability to work single-mindedly on your most important task will contribute as much to your success as any other discipline you can develop.

5. *Daily exercise and proper nutrition:* Your health is more important than anything else. By disciplining yourself to exercise regularly and to eat carefully, you will promote the highest possible levels of health and fitness throughout your life.

6. *Daily learning and growth:* Your mind is like a muscle. If you don't use it, you lose it. Continuous learning is the minimum requirement for success in any field.

7. *Daily time for the important people in your life:* Relationships are everything. Be sure that in climbing the ladder of success, you do not find it leaning against the wrong building. Build time for your relationships into every day, no matter how busy you get.

These seven disciplines will ensure that you perform at the highest level and get the greatest satisfaction and results from everything you do.

The 1,000 Percent Formula

There is a simple, practical, proven self-development formula that you can use to double your income in the years ahead. It's a formula I developed early in my career, which proved effective, and I have passed it on to thousands of people. The only complaint I have ever received on this formula is that it is too conservative.

Most people who practice this formula each day report extraordinary improvements in their lives. These changes take place quickly, often within a couple of days. Try it and see for yourself.

This 1,000 percent formula is based on the law of incremental improvement. This law says that "by the yard it's hard, but inch by inch, anything's a cinch."

No matter how excited or determined you are, change and progress take place slowly. It takes you your entire life to become the person you are. It takes a period of hard work and determination to become someone different. We do not usually make significant and lasting changes in quantum leaps. All permanent change is progressive, over a long period of time. This type of change takes patience and discipline. It is only this type of change that is truly worthwhile and enduring.

Here is a question for you: Is it possible for you to increase your overall productivity, performance, and output by 0.1 percent in the next 24 hours?

In other words, could you become one-thousandth (0.1 percent) more productive over the next twenty-four hours if you really wanted to? The truth is that you could probably become 0.1 percent more productive right now, in a couple of minutes, just by working on a single high-value task.

By setting goals and priorities and by focusing on higher-value activities, anyone can increase his or her overall productivity and performance by 1/1,000 over the next twenty-four hours. Many people could double or triple their overall productivity in the next twenty-four hours if they really wanted to.

If you continually learn, study, and upgrade your skills, clarify and reclarify your goals, set better and clearer priorities, and focus on progressively more valuable tasks, you can increase your overall productivity performance and output by 0.1 percent each day, day after day, indefinitely.

Because of the law of increasing returns introduced in Chapter One, every effort you make to be more productive in one area tends to improve your performance in every other area at the same time. You will get better and better results, in less time, the more you practice.

If you become 0.1 percent more productive each day, five days per week, at the end of a week you will be 0.5 percent more productive. At the end of four weeks, you will be 2 percent more productive ($4 \times 0.5 = 2$). At the end of fifty-two weeks, you will be 26 percent more productive than you were at the beginning of the year ($13 \times 2 = 26$).

This is where the compounding effect of new knowledge and skill begins to work. Every improvement in any part of your work affects other parts of your work at the same time. As you become better at managing your time, you will become more productive with your customers and clients. As you become more productive with your customers and clients, you will become more competent and effective in other parts of your business. Each improvement leads to other improvements.

By becoming 26 percent more productive over the course of a year and continuing to improve by 0.1 percent per day, five days a week, you will double your overall productivity, performance, and output in 2.7 years. If you continue learning, growing, and becoming more effective and efficient, an improvement of 26 percent per year, compounded over ten years, will result in an increase of 1,004 percent in your overall productivity.

Because we live in a merit-based society, as you increase your ability to contribute value, the amount you earn will increase as well. If you improve your overall performance by 1,004 percent, your income eventually will rise to match the value of your contribution.

Many students have come back to me after four, five, or six years and told me that they were able to increase their incomes by 1,000 percent in just a few years by practicing this formula. In every case, they were astonished at how quickly they had moved to the top of their fields by the simple act of making small, incremental improvements each day.

Here are the seven steps in the 1,000 percent formula that will help you become 0.1 percent better daily, 0.5 percent better each week, 2 percent better each month, and 26 percent better each year.

■ Arise two hours before your first appointment and read for one hour in your field. This is called the Golden Hour, and it sets the tone for the rest of the day. Leave the television off, put the newspaper aside. Invest the first sixty minutes in yourself and in your mind. This first hour is the rudder of your day.

■ Rewrite and review your major goals each day before you start off. Take a few minutes to write out your goals in a spiral notebook, in the present tense, as though you had already achieved them. This programs your subconscious mind to be alert to opportunities to achieve your goals all day long.

■ Plan every day in advance. Make a list of everything you have to do the night before, before you end your work day or before you go to bed. This enables your subconscious mind to work on your list while you sleep. Often, when you awake, you will have ideas and insights that will enable you to achieve your daily goals faster and more effectively.

■ Always concentrate on the most valuable use of your time. Select the one task that can have the greatest positive impact on your work life, and begin on that task first thing in the morning.

■ Listen to educational audio programs in your car. Turn your car into a mobile classroom, a university on wheels. This activity is so powerful that it alone can give you your 1,000 percent increase in the years ahead.

■ Ask two questions after every experience. These questions enable you to learn and grow more rapidly from everything that happens to you: What did I do right? and What would I do differently?

According to the law of concentration, whatever you dwell upon grows in your experience. Whatever you pay attention to increases in your life. Whatever you focus on, you tend to do better. When you analyze each experience by asking, "What did I do right?" and "What would I do differently?" you program yourself to perform even better in each subsequent experience. These questions enable you to extract the maximum number of lessons out of each thing you do. They enable you to learn at an accelerated rate.

The best news of all is that when you are concentrating on what you did right and what you would do differently, your mind becomes positive, productive, and creative. You become more motivated and more eager to try new things. You become even more likely to apply the insights you derived from your previous experiences.

■ The seventh and final ingredient on the 1,000 percent formula is for you to treat everyone you meet like a million-dollar customer. Treat the people you work with the same way you would treat a valuable customer of your firm. Treat each prospect or customer as if that person had already purchased $1 million of your company's product or service and was thinking of doing it again. Also, treat the people at home as though they were the most valuable people in the world to you, because they are.

Make Your Personal Growth and Development Action Commitment

You are your most precious resource. Your earning ability is your most valuable asset. Invest every day in improving yourself as a person and increasing your ability to earn even more. Most people who are earning $250,000 today started off earning $25,000 or less.

Decide today to develop yourself to the point where you can achieve every financial and personal goal you ever set and become everything you are capable of becoming.

CHAPTER ELEVEN

Make a Difference in Your Community

The best thing about giving of ourselves is that what we get is always better than what we give. The reaction is greater than the action.

—ORISON SWETT MARDEN

You were born to do something wonderful with your life. There has never been and never will be anyone just like you. You are unique. Your special combination of talents, abilities, emotions, ideas, attitudes, and philosophy makes you distinct from all other beings who will ever live.

You have extraordinary potential talents and abilities that you do not use. You have an incredible brain, composed of as many as 100 billion cells. Each of these cells is connected and interconnected with as many as 20,000 other cells. The possible combinations of thoughts and ideas that you can have are greater than the number of molecules in the known universe. You are truly extraordinary!

One of the most important questions you can ever ask and answer is this: "What kind of difference do I want to make with my life?"

What do you want to be famous for? How do you want people to think about you and talk about you when you are gone? What kind of mark do you want to leave on the world? What do you want to do that will improve the lives of other people?

In his writings, Peter Drucker tells about a high school teacher who advised his students to begin thinking of the legacy they wanted to leave when they passed on. Even though they were only in their late teens, he advised them that it was not too early to begin thinking of leaving a legacy.

Ten years later, at a class reunion, Drucker met with some of the students in that class. It turned out that a few of them had taken that message to heart and had already begun thinking of leaving a legacy when they started their careers. Those students, he found, had reached far higher levels of success in their careers than had the other students who had not given the idea of leaving a legacy much thought.

These young men were different from the others in their orientation toward themselves and their world. They had higher levels of self-esteem and self-respect. They were more serious and self-confident. The thought of leaving a legacy had influenced their thinking and affected their decision making for several years.

What kind of legacy do you want to leave? In his best-selling book *The 7 Habits of Highly Effective People,* Stephen

Covey says that the four great goals of life are "to live, to love, to learn and to leave a legacy." It seems that most of the great men and women of history have given a good deal of thought to the contribution they wanted to make to their society.

Peter Daniels, an Australian businessperson, read more than 500 biographies and autobiographies of famous men and women. He found that these men and women all had one thing in common. He called it a "sense of destiny."

Throughout history, men and women who have left a real mark on their societies have believed that their lives had a special meaning. They believed that they were put on Earth to do some great thing that would benefit mankind.

Albert Schweitzer was one of the greatest humanitarians in history. When he was thirty years old, in the late 1800s, he was the top Bach organist in Europe. He was the equivalent of a musical superstar today. He played in the great concert halls in the great capital cities of Europe. He was highly respected and extremely successful.

And yet at age 30 he began thinking about making a greater difference with his life. At that time, at the end of the nineteenth century, Africa was just opening up. There were many stories in the newspapers and magazines describing the sufferings and privations of the native peoples.

Albert Schweitzer decided to become a medical missionary. To that end, he went back to school and devoted eight years of his life to earning a degree in tropical medicine. He played concerts on the side to raise money. At age 38, he loaded his medical supplies on a ship and sailed to Africa. He transferred his supplies to a small boat and traveled up the Oogoouè River to a thatched village called Lambarene. There, he set up his tent and began his work.

By the time he died, fifty-three years later, at age 91, his village hospital had grown to a population of 1,500 people, with forty medical doctors and specialists drawn from all over the world. Within ten years of his death, there were more hospitals in the world named after him than any other person. He left a legacy that will last a hundred years, and perhaps forever.

Mother Theresa, of the Missionaries of Charity in Calcutta, was the greatest humanitarian of her age as well. She dedicated her entire life to working with the poor and dying people of India. Her message of unconditional love and acceptance had a profound effect on everyone who met her and on many millions who knew about her only from reading or from seeing her on television. She was a remarkable person. She left an extraordinary legacy that goes on to this day.

Determine Your Humanitarian Values

In leaving a legacy and making a difference with your life in your community, begin with your values. These may be spiritual values, economic values, social values, personal values, human values, or any values at all that you consider to be important and relevant to the human condition. You may be motivated by love, compassion, freedom, faith, kindness, sympathy, courage, or generosity. What moves you emotionally to give of yourself and your resources?

Look at your community and your nation. What causes, organizations, movements, or schools of belief are you attracted to? What kind of contribution would you like to make with your life? If you were extraordinarily wealthy, what causes would you contribute to? What changes would you like to see in your society that would be beneficial to other people?

Bill and Melissa Gates of Microsoft have formed the Bill and Melissa Gates Foundation, endowed with $40 billion. One focal point of their charitable activities is inoculations and vaccinations against dangerous diseases for children around the world, especially in undeveloped countries. They have decided that one way in which they can make a significant difference in the world is to ensure that these children live to adulthood so that they can become active members of their communities.

Many people contribute their time and money to their churches and spiritual activities. Others are committed to making a difference politically or economically. Many men and women are committed to improving educational opportunities for children or to teaching literacy to adults. Some people are committed to the environment and others to population control.

The one factor these people all have in common seems to be passion. People who make a significant difference in their worlds all seem to have a great passion for what they are doing and what they espouse. They are often willing to suffer tremendous privation and make incredible sacrifices to promote their ideals. They believe deeply in the rightness and goodness of what they stand for and are willing to go great distances to promote their causes.

Herodotus once wrote, "All of life is action and passion. Not to be involved with the actions and passions of your time is to run the risk of having not really lived at all."

What is your passion? What problems or needs in your society do you really care about? What do you find yourself naturally attracted to and interested in? What sort of issues do you find yourself discussing, arguing, and debating? In what areas do you have strong feelings about what should be done or should not be done?

Viktor Frankl, founder of Logotherapy and author of the book *Man's Search for Meaning,* survived the Nazi death camps of World War II. During this time he had a profound revelation. He found that the strongest driving force in the human psyche is the need for meaning and purpose, an intense desire to be committed to something bigger than oneself. Frankl concluded that each person needs to be able to commit to a cause that is greater than he or she is. Each of us needs to be dedicated to something that benefits other people in some way. We need to be able to rise above ourselves, to get out of ourselves, and to put our hearts into doing something that makes a difference in the world and in the lives of others.

Clarify Your Vision of a Perfect World

What is your vision of a perfect world? If the world were ideal in an area of great concern to you, what would it look like? Imagine that you could wave a magic wand and bring about the perfect situation. What would it look like?

When I was working with a committee in Washington that had been commissioned by Congress to develop solutions to a perplexing national problem, we began with a simple question: "If we were completely successful and all our recommendations were accepted, what would America look like five or ten years in the future?"

We spent several hours imagining and envisioning an America that was ideal in every respect. We then discussed and voted on which elements of this vision were most important. We organized these ideal elements in terms of priorities, from the most important to the least important. At the end of this process, we had a shared vision of exactly what we were working toward. We then went to work on the problem, produced a series of thoughtful recommendations and conclusions, and submitted the report to Congress. It turned out to be a tremendous success.

When I work with nonprofit organizations, we always start off with a vision statement. In this vision statement, we ask, "What is our mission?"

We ask, "If we were completely successful in achieving our mission, how would we know? What would it look like? What would happen? What goals would we have to achieve for us to be able to disband this organization and go home, content that we had been successful?"

Look around you in your society. There are many nonprofit organizations, aimed at achieving a variety of social goals, that need your help. Don't make the mistake of putting off getting involved until you have lots of money. Invest your time and energy until you are in a position to invest your money in the organizations you believe in. Give of your time and emotion to a cause you consider important today. Make this practice of contributing a regular part of your life.

Set Goals for Your Charitable Contributions

What are your goals for the type and level of contribution you want to make to society? If you had an unlimited amount of money, what would you want to do or achieve with that money in terms of improving your society or your community? How would you measure success?

Andrew Carnegie, the great steel magnate, who started as a penniless day laborer in a Pittsburgh steel plant, sold his steel interests in 1895 for $595 million at a time when there were no income taxes.

Throughout his life, he had a simple philosophy. It was to spend the first part of his life making a lot of money and then to spend the second part of his life giving it all away. He was famous for having said, "He who dies rich dies dishonored."

For the rest of his life, he built libraries and set up foundations to help people to learn what they needed to learn to be successful and happy. By the time he died, he had given almost all his money away. Today, the Carnegie foundations and libraries that bear his name stand as a magnificent tribute to one of the greatest businesspeople and philanthropists of American history.

John D. Rockefeller, who became the richest man in the world, started as a clerk at $3.75 per week. Even at that small salary, he gave as much as 50 percent of his salary to his church every week to contribute to the betterment of others.

Years passed. When he was fifty-two years old, he was extraordinarily wealthy, perhaps the richest man in the world. He was also extremely sick, and his doctors told him that he would die within a year.

He thought back on his early years and the pleasure he got from contributing to his church. He resolved that he would spend his last year giving his money away. He sold half of his stock in the Standard Oil Company. He then began financing worthy causes around the country.

Something incredible happened. The more money he gave away, the better he felt. His health improved. His illnesses went away. He recovered completely. He went on to live to age 91, in cxccllent health.

By the time he died, he had given away millions of dollars. Meanwhile, the value of the Standard Oil Stock he had kept had increased so much that he died with more money than he had had when he was on his deathbed many years before.

Become a Wise and Knowledgable Giver

What additional knowledge and skills will you need to make a difference in your community? Money that is given away at random usually is of little value. Money contributed by an informed donor usually is far more effective at achieving important social goals.

You probably have heard that you should "investigate before you invest." You should also investigate before you contribute your time or your funds to any worthy cause. Do your homework. Do research on organizations that you are thinking about contributing to. Make sure the money you donate is being spent on a good cause rather than on salaries, benefits, and additional fundraising expenses.

If you want to work personally for a particular charity, identify the most important skills you need to develop to maximize the value of the time you donate. Many people see their charitable activities as an opportunity for personal growth and development. Just as they are committed to becoming better and better in their work, they are also committed to becoming better and better at making a valuable contribution of their time and effort to worthy causes.

The principle of tithing, or giving 10 percent of your income to worthy causes, has been advocated for thousands of years. Many people feel that tithing unleashes a flood of benefits, both financial and otherwise, into your life. However, tithing can also refer to the amount of time you invest in your community. Giving of yourself often is more important than giving money. The best is a combination of both, but if your funds are limited, contribute your time instead to the causes you believe in.

Develop the Qualities and Habits You Need

Identify the specific habits that will enable you to make a significant contribution to society. You may want to develop the habits of self-discipline, self-denial, diligence, wisdom, foresight, patience, and humility. It is amazing how much you can get done if nobody cares who gets the credit.

Create Your Daily Schedule for Social Contribution

What daily activities would you engage in if you wanted to make a contribution to worthy causes? What would you do regularly to ensure that you were making a genuine difference in the quality of your community? Would you be attending meetings? Making telephone calls? Writing letters? Serving on church or community boards or committees?

It is often said that the more you give of yourself without expectation of reward, the more rewards will come back to you from the most unexpected sources.

When you dedicate yourself to serving others, to working for a cause that is greater than yourself, you receive profound emotional and spiritual benefits that can be much greater and more important than any material rewards you could imagine.

One of the great secrets of success is for you to always do what you love to do. It is for you to find something that fascinates you and attracts you. You can then put your whole heart into doing it extremely well.

When you find a cause you really care about and you begin putting your whole heart into that cause, making a difference in your society and your community, you feel terrific about yourself. You feel happy and fulfilled. You feel important and valuable to yourself and to your world. You unlock more and more of your potential and become more and more of what you are meant to be. You move into a position of true leadership.

Back Your Good Intentions with Specific Actions

Decide today to make a specific action commitment, to do something that makes a difference. It may be something as simple as making a financial contribution to an organization or cause you believe in. It may be calling an individual or organization and volunteering your services. It may be setting a goal to do something that can have a profound impact on people in the years ahead. Whatever it is, do it now.

CHAPTER TWELVE

Spiritual Development and Inner Peace

It is only with the heart that one can see rightly; what is essential is invisible to the eye.

—ANTOINE DE SAINT-EXUPÉRY

S piritual development and understanding have been the goals of great minds throughout human history. In every culture, society, and civilization, spiritual traditions have emerged and developed spontaneously without any external input or influence, often many thousands of miles apart.

We all seem to have a desire to connect with something higher and greater than ourselves. This inner drive seems to arise naturally and normally, often without any guidance or instruction. The great mystics and spiritual teachers of human history are those who have emerged to teach people how they can best satisfy this spiritual craving.

The whole issue of spiritual development is complex and controversial. Each person who believes in a faith or a denomination usually is convinced that his or her ideas about God or a higher power are correct, and all others are wrong or misguided to some degree.

Among the most terrible wars in human history have been religious wars fought over differences in dogma, doctrine, or interpretation. Because most religions preach that God is a God of love, compassion, and understanding, it is sometimes amazing to look at what has been done, and what continues to be done, in the name of God.

I have studied spiritual traditions for more than thirty years. I very much believe that spiritual development is the highest and most important form of development a person can pursue. Rightly understood, spiritual development is the key to peace, prosperity, happiness, and personal fulfillment.

About 325 B.C., Aristotle wrote his "Nicomachean Ethics," one of history's finest explanations of the human condition. He began with the observation that the common denominator of humankind is the desire to be happy. He concluded that the question of how to achieve this happiness is the fundamental question of philosophy.

In 1895, Sigmund Freud of Vienna introduced his theory of psychoanalysis. His fundamental conclusion followed directly from Aristotle, more than 2,000 years before. He called it the Pleasure Principle.

Freud taught that human beings are motivated to move toward pleasure and to avoid pain, to move toward comfort and away from discomfort—physical, emotional, financial, or of any other kind.

Modern economists and psychologists agree that every human action is stimulated by a felt dissatisfaction of some kind. Without this felt dissatisfaction, no action takes place. The person remains content and satisfied.

The primary driving forces of human behavior begin with discontent, dissatisfaction, discomfort, or unhappiness. Action takes place when the person perceives a better state or condition where this unhappiness or discontent can be relieved. The person then acts to achieve this goal. The action is either successful or unsuccessful. But all human behavior is aimed at achieving a higher state of happiness than the one that currently exists.

The Highest Human Good

The highest human good is peace of mind. In fact, you can measure the success of your life at any given time by your level of happiness and peace of mind, by how good you feel about yourself and your world.

Peace of mind is possible only when you feel completely satisfied and content inside. Peace of mind comes when you follow your intuition, your inner voice, and you do and say the things that feel exactly right for you.

No one can determine what will make another person happy. Because each person is unique, each person has different needs and desires and is motivated by different goals and results. Each of us can decide only for ourselves what makes us happy. And each of us can decide what makes us happy only by listening to our inner voice and following its guidance and direction.

All religious traditions seem to have in common a series of simple principles. The first principle is that there is a higher power or being who loves us, knows us, understands us, and wants the very best for us.

It doesn't matter what it is called. It is a comforting thought to believe and accept that there is a great power in the universe that we can turn to, that desires our good, and that will guide us to do and say the right things if we listen to the voice within us.

Intuition is one of the greatest gifts of humankind. Every great thinker has been amazed at this wonderful power. And the more you listen to your intuition, the better and more accurate it becomes. The more you listen to your inner voice, the louder and clearer it becomes in guiding you to make the right decisions in each area of your life.

The Practice of Solitude

One of the great spiritual practices is that of solitude and contemplation. Many people have never tried the practice of solitude, but it is an extraordinarily positive experience. French mathematician and philosopher Blaise Pascal wrote, "Almost all the problems of mankind arise from the inability to be alone with oneself in a room for any period of time."

If ever you desire an answer to any question, a solution to any dilemma, or the resolution to any difficulty, practice solitude. Go and sit quietly by yourself, with no noise or distractions, for sixty minutes. It has been said that men and women begin to become great when they begin to spend time alone with themselves, listening to their inner voices.

During this period of solitude, your mind will clear. After about thirty minutes of quiet contemplation, you will feel calm and relaxed. You will feel happy and peaceful. You will feel at one with the universe. And then, at a certain moment, as you sit there, ideas and insights will begin to flow through your mind.

Whatever your current situation, the right answer for you will come to you at exactly the right time in exactly the right form. When you arise from your period of solitude and take action on that answer, you will find that it is exactly the right thing to do. This is the height of spiritual perception and spiritual connection.

The Golden Rule

Another principle spiritual traditions have in common is the Golden Rule: Do unto others as you would have them do unto you. It was a wise person who wrote, "There may be a better principle for human living than the Golden Rule, but no one has yet discovered it."

The great truths of life are simple. It is amazing how many problems, both personal and social, could be resolved if everyone decided to treat other people the way they would like to be treated. Listen to people the way you would like to be listened to. Sell your products and services the way you would like others to sell their products and services to you. Be courteous and respectful to other people, just as you would like them to be courteous and respectful to you. Be patient and understanding with people when they make mistakes, just as you would like them to be patient and understanding with you when you make mistakes.

The Universal Maxim

Another principle common to religious traditions was best articulated by German philosopher Immanuel Kant. He called it the universal maxim: "Live your life as though your every act were to become a universal law."

This is an amazing idea! Imagine if everyone lived and behaved as if everyone else was going to do exactly what he or she did. Imagine that everyone was going to treat other people exactly the way you treat them.

This universal maxim is a tremendous guide for individual behavior. It harms no one and it helps everyone. It requires truthfulness, honesty, and justice. The universal maxim requires that we treat everyone alike. Living by the universal maxim requires the utmost spiritual and personal discipline.

Four Great Questions

Here are four questions that you can ask and answer for yourself regularly. They help you incorporate the universal maxim into your life.

1. *What kind of world would it be if everyone in it were just like me?* Most of the problems in the world today could be solved if everyone could say that this would be a better world if everyone behaved as they do.

2. *What kind of country would my country be if everyone in it were just like me?* Most of our social and political problems are a direct result of people's refusal to ask this question about themselves, about others, and about our country.

3. *What kind of company would my company be if everyone in it were just like me?* This is one of the best questions for creating a terrific place to work. The more peo-

ple there are in a company who can answer this question positively, the better company it becomes in every way.

4. *What kind of family would my family be if everyone in it were just like me?* Imagine everyone in your family treated one another the way you treat them. What kind of family would it be?

Each of us is a work in progress. Each of us has a long way to go. Each of us has ample room for improvement. There are many things each of us can do to become better human beings and better members of society. Asking ourselves these four questions regularly gives us guidance and insights into the specific changes and improvements we can make.

Determine Your Spiritual Values

What are your values with regard to spiritual development? Do you believe in the values of peace, joy, love, compassion, forgiveness, self-control, faith, hope, happiness, and personal fulfillment?

Select the values you consider to be most important from the Appendix. Organize your values by priority, from most important to least important. Put an "X" on your most important value and then begin to think about how you could express this value more often in your words and actions.

Discipline yourself to live your life in harmony with your most important spiritual value. Whenever you slip, catch yourself and begin living according to this value once again. In time, you will program this value into your subconscious mind. You will instill this value as a permanent part of your personality. You will actually transform your character. You will become a better person in every sense of the word.

Clarify Your Spiritual Vision

What is your vision for complete peace of mind? If your inner life were perfect in every way, and you were completely happy and fulfilled, how would you be living your life?

Think back over the happiest moments of your life. Think about the times when you felt the greatest joy and inner peace. What was going on? Who were you with? What were you doing? What have been your most joyous experiences in life? What could you do to create a situation in which you could enjoy more of those happy experiences in the year ahead?

What should your focal point be? What one change or decision could you make that would move you more rapidly to a higher level of spiritual and inner development, a higher level of happiness and peace?

Practice zero-based thinking. Look at your life and ask yourself whether there is anything you are doing that, knowing what you now know, you wouldn't get into again today.

Is there any relationship, personal or business, that you wouldn't get into again today if you had to do it over? Is there any part of your business, any product, service, process, or activity that you would not start up again today, knowing what you now know?

Is there any investment or drain on your time, emotion, energy, or money that you would not get into again today if you had to do it over, knowing what you now know?

Sometimes, the decision to stop doing something that is no longer a source of joy or happiness in your life can bring you more peace and satisfaction than anything else. And you usually know what it is.

The only question is whether you have the courage and character to take the action that you know you need to take.

Set Your Spiritual Goals

What are your goals for spiritual and inner development? What specific, measurable steps can you take to achieve higher levels of happiness and personal satisfaction? What can you do today to eliminate the people, forces, and influences in your life that are disrupting your happiness and peace of mind?

Remember that there are only four ways to bring about the changes you desire. You can do more of some things, or you can do less of others. You can start doing something, or you can stop doing something else altogether. Which is it to be?

Develop New Spiritual Habits

What habits and behaviors do you need to develop to become a happier person and to enjoy greater peace of mind in everything you do?

Many people develop the habit of reading spiritually each morning and thinking about how they can practice what they read during the day. Others develop the habit of daily solitude. Some develop the habit of attending church. One spiritual habit is to donate your time to working with people who are less fortunate than you are. Spending time with other spiritually developed people is another great habit that helps you to develop spiritually.

Create Your Daily Spiritual Activity Schedule

Identify the daily activities you could begin practicing to increase your levels of spiritual development and inner peace. Whatever you do, anything that you repeat eventually will become a new habit. What are the specific activities that you would like to develop into habits?

Make Your Spiritual Action Commitment

Next, make a specific action commitment. Choose one step you are going to take today to begin moving toward higher levels of spiritual development and peace of mind. Either start doing something or stop doing something else. Make a decision of some kind and then take action on your decision.

Determine your focal point. Put an "X" on the one decision or activity that can have the most immediate positive impact on your level of personal happiness and inner joy.

The Path to Spiritual Development

Perhaps the most important spiritual principle is an unshakable trust in the universe and the goodness of a higher power or being.

Look for the good in every situation. Look for something beneficial that you can gain from every setback or difficulty. Have complete faith that everything that is happening to you is happening for a good reason. Whatever is happening at the moment usually will help you to be more successful and happy in the future if you are willing to learn from it.

Norman Vincent Peale used to say, "When God wants to send you a gift, he wraps it up in a problem. The bigger the gift that God wants to send you, the bigger the problem he wraps it up in."

In a project that involved interviews with hundreds of the most successful men and women of our age, researchers found that they all had a single quality in common. They all believed that, in every difficulty and problem they faced, there was something good or beneficial that they could benefit from.

Look for the valuable lesson in every difficulty. Have complete faith that there is a divine intelligence that cares about you and is guiding your path every step of the way. When you begin practicing this way of thinking, you will be amazed at the wonderful things that happen in your life.

Identify the biggest single problem in your life today. Look into that problem and imagine that it has been sent to you to teach you something you need to know. Imagine that this problem has been artfully constructed to contain one or more valuable lessons that you absolutely need to learn to move to the next level of success and happiness in your life.

All the great people I have known are men and women of faith. They have complete confidence that everything is unfolding for their good, even if they cannot see it at the moment. They believe that every setback has a benefit or opportunity hidden within it. They have complete faith that everything is happening as it should and that at the end, everything will turn out well. And they are seldom disappointed.

No Higher Aim

Spiritual development and peace of mind are the highest of all human goods and benefits. Spiritual development enhances your life and fills you with joy and satisfaction. It makes you happy and gives you tremendous pleasure. Best of all, it is available to everyone at no cost.

Developing spiritually and enjoying peace of mind simply means living in truth with yourself and with everyone around you. Spiritual development means trusting in the universe to guide and direct your path. Spiritual development means taking time each day to sit quietly by yourself and listening for the still, small voice within. Spiritual development means following the guidance of your intuition and believing that everything is working out for the best.

When you begin to live in truth with yourself and others and trust your inner voice, you will make your life something truly wonderful and inspiring. And it's completely up to you.

Seven Lessons for the Twenty-First Century

H ere are seven lessons for success in the twenty-first century. These are some of the most important ideas I have learned in more than thirty years of studying successful people.

1. *Your life only gets better when you get better.* Your outer world will always reflect your inner world. If you want to improve the quality of your outer world, you must work on yourself. And because there is no limit to how much better you can get, there is no limit to how much better you can make your life.

2. *It doesn't matter where you're coming from; all that matters is where you're going.* Never allow yourself to be slowed down or held back by events that have occurred in your past. Learn from them and let them go. Resolve to keep yourself focused on the future and where you are going. Because your future is limited only by your imagination, there are no limits to what you can achieve in the months and years ahead.

3. *Anything worth doing well is worth doing poorly at first.* Everything is hard before it is easy. A primary reason that people do not realize their full potential is that they try something new, and when it doesn't work perfectly the first time they quit and go back to their old, lower level of performance. Anything worth doing well is worth doing poorly at first, and it is often worth doing poorly several times until you master it.

4. *You are only as free as your options, the well-developed alternatives you have available to you.* One of the greatest human goods is personal freedom, and your freedom is determined largely by your choices. The more options you have, the greater freedom and self-confidence you have. You should be continually developing new options throughout your career. Never hang all your hopes for success on a single possibility.

5. *Within every problem or difficulty you experience, there is the seed of an equal or greater advantage or benefit.* Look for the good in every problem. Look for the valuable lesson in every adversity or setback. Look for something you can gain from every difficulty, and you will always find it.

6. *You can learn anything you need to learn to achieve any goal you can set for yourself.* You are a learning organism. Anything that anyone else has learned, within reason, you can learn as well. You can acquire any kind of knowledge and develop any skill you need to rise to the top of your field.

7. *The only real limits on what you can do or be are the limits you accept in your own mind.* As Shakespeare said, "Nothing is, but thinking makes it so." Henry Ford said, "If you believe you can do a thing or you believe you cannot, in either case, you are probably right."

You have within you, right now, all the talents and abilities you could ever want or need to achieve any goal or dream you can set for yourself. The only question you ever have to ask is, "How badly do I want it?"

If you want anything badly enough and you are willing to persist long enough, nothing can stop you from achieving it.

Good luck!

Focal Point Advanced Coaching and Mentoring Program

Brian Tracy offers a personal coaching program in San Diego for successful entrepreneurs, self-employed professionals, and top salespeople. Participants learn how to apply the Focal Point Process to every part of their work and personal lives.

Participants learn a step-by-step process of personal strategic planning that enables them to take complete control of their time and their lives. Over the course of the program, participants meet with Brian Tracy one full day every three months. During these sessions, they learn how to double their income and double their time off.

They identify the things they enjoy doing the most and learn how to become better in their most profitable activities. Participants learn how to delegate, downsize, eliminate, and get rid of all the tasks they neither enjoy nor benefit from. They learn how to identify their special talents and how to use leverage and concentration to move to the top of their fields.

For more information on the Coaching and Mentoring Program, visit http://www.briantracy.com, call 858-481-2977, or write to Brian Tracy International, 462 Stevens Road, Solana Beach, CA, 92075.

List of Values

Accuracy
Achievement
Adaptability
Adventure
Affection
Alertness
Ambition
Assertiveness
Authenticity
Balance
Beauty
Boldness
Broad-mindedness
Calmness
Capability
Career
Caring
Clear thinking
Compassion
Competence
Confidence

Conscientiousness
Consideration
Contentment
Contribution
Cooperation
Courage
Creativity
Customer service
Dependability
Determination
Diligence
Discipline
Dynamism
Education
Effectiveness
Encouragement
Energy
Enjoyment
Enterprise
Enthusiasm
Excellence

Faith   Love
Fitness   Loyalty
Flexibility   Maturity
Focus   Method
Forgiveness   Meticulousness
Freedom   Modesty
Friendship   Naturalness
Fulfillment   Nurturing
Generosity   Optimism
Gentleness   Organization
Good attitude   Originality
Good humor   Patience
Growth   Peace
Happiness   Perseverance
Hard work   Persistence
Health   Personal fulfillment
Helpfulness   Personal mastery
Honesty   Playfulness
Hope   Pleasantness
Humility   Politeness
Imagination   Possessiveness
Impartiality   Practicality
Independence   Precision
Innovation   Professionalism
Integrity   Progress
Joviality   Prosperity
Joy   Punctuality
Kindness   Purposefulness
Knowledge   Quality
Leadership   Quickness
Learning   Resourcefulness

Respect

Responsibility

Satisfaction

Security

Self-actualization

Self-control

Sensibility

Simplicity

Sincerity

Skill

Sociability

Specialness

Status

Strength

Success

Sympathy

Tact

Talent

Teamwork

Thankfulness

Thoroughness

Tolerance

Tranquility

Trustworthiness

Truthfulness

Understanding

Uniqueness

Value

Versatility

Victory

Vigor

Warmth

Willpower

Wisdom

Wit

Youthfulness

Zeal

Recommended Reading

Caplan, Robert S., and David P. Norton, *The Balanced Score Card*, Harvard Business School Press, 1996.

Covey, Stephen, *The 7 Habits of Highly Effective People*, Fireside, 1990.

Covey, Stephen, *First Things First*, Fireside, 1998.

De Angelis, Barbara, *How to Make Love All the Time*, Dell Books, 1997.

De Angelis, Barbara, *Ask Barbara: The 100 Most Asked Questions About Love, Sex, and Relationships*, Dell Books, 1998.

Drucker, Peter, *Essential Drucker: In One Volume, the Best of Sixty Years of Peter Drucker's Essential Writings on Management*, New York, Harperbusiness, 2001.

Drucker, Peter, *Management Challenges of the 21st Century*, New York, Harperbusiness, 2001.

Drucker, Peter, *The Effective Executive*, Harperbusiness, 1993.

Goleman, Daniel, *Emotional Intelligance*, Bantam Books, 1997.

Greenleaf, Robert K., *Servant Leadership*, Paulist Press, 1977.

Grove, Andrew, *High Output Management*, Vintage, 1995.

Hill, Napoleon, *Think and Grow Rich*, Fawcett Books, 1990.

Hill, Napoleon, *Napoleon Hill's Keys to Success: The 17 Principles of Personal Achievement*, Plume, 1997.

Hubbard, Elbert, *Elbert Hubbard's Scrap Book: Containing the Inspired and Inspiring Selections Gathered During a Life Time of Discriminating Reading for His Own Use*, Firebird Press, 1999.

Hubbard, Elbert, *A Message to Garcia*, Firebird Press, 1983.

Krass, Peter, *The Book of Business Wisdom*, Wiley, 1997.

Land, George, and Beth Jarman, *Break-Point and Beyond*, Harperbusiness, 1992.

Lynch, Peter, *One Up on Wall Street, How to Use What You Already Know to Make Money in the Market*, Simon & Schuster, 2000.

Orman, Suzie, *The 9 Steps to Financial Freedom*, Crown, 1997.

Peale, Norman Vincent, *The Power of Positive Thinking*, Ballantine Books, 1996.

Qubein, Nido R., *Stairway to Success*, Executive Books, 1996.

Riley, Pat, *The Winner Within, A Life Plan for Team Players*, Berkley Publishing Group, 1994.

Seligman, Martin E. P., *Learned Optimism: How to Change Your Mind and Your Life*, Pocket Books, 1998.

Smith, Hyrum, *What Matters Most*, Simon & Schuster, 2000.

Slater, Robert, *Jack Welch and the G. E. Way: Management Insights and Leadership Secrets of the Legendary CEO*, McGraw-Hill, 1998.

Stanley, Thomas, *The Millionaire Mind*, Andrews McMeel, 2000.

Stanley, Thomas, and William D. Danko, *The Millionaire Next Door*, Longstreet, 1996.

Tracy, Brian, *Maximum Achievement*, Simon & Schuster, 1990.

Tracy, Brian, *Advanced Selling Strategies*, Simon & Schuster, 1993.

Tracy, Brian, *The 100 Absolutely Unbreakable Laws of Business Success*, Berrett-Koehler, 2000.

Tracy, Brian, *The 21 Success Secrets of Self-Made Millionaires*, Berrett-Koehler, 2000.

Tracy, Brian, *Eat That Frog! 21 Great Ways to Stop Procrastinating and Get More Things Done Sooner*, Berrett-Koehler, 2001.

Tracy, Brian, *Get Paid More and Promoted Faster—21 Ways to Accelerate Your Career*, Berrett-Koehler, 2001.

Trout, Jack, *The Power of Simplicity*, McGraw Hill, 1999.

I N D E X

ABOUT THE AUTHOR

Brian Tracy is one of the top professional speakers in the world. He addresses more than 450,000 people each year throughout the United States, Canada, Europe, Australia, and Asia.

His keynote speeches, talks, and seminars are customized for each audience. They have been described as "inspiring, entertaining, informative, and motivational." He has worked with more than 500 corporations, given more than 2,000 talks, and addressed millions of people.

Some of his speech topics include the following:

Leadership in the New Millennium: How to be a more effective leader in every area of business life. Learn the most powerful, practical leadership strategies ever discovered to manage, motivate, and get better results than ever before.

21st-Century Thinking: How to outthink, outplan, and outperform your competition. How to get superior results in a fast-moving, fast-changing business environment.

The Psychology of Peak Performance: How the top people think and act in every area of personal and business life. Learn a series of practical, proven methods and strategies for maximum achievement.

Superior Selling Strategies: How to sell more, faster, and easier to demanding customers in highly competitive markets. How to sell higher-priced products and services against lower-priced competitors.

For full information on booking Brian Tracy to speak at your next meeting or conference, visit http://www.briantracy.com, call 858-481-2977, or write to Brian Tracy International, 462 Stevens Road, Solana Beach, CA, 92075.